The Children's Bristol Series

24 Family Walks

IN AND AROUND BRISTOL

Lesley Turney

First published in the Children's Bristol Series in 2006 by Redcliffe Press Ltd.,
81g Pembroke Road, Bristol BS8 3EA

ISBN 1 904537 47 2
ISBN 13 978 1904537 47 2

www.childrensbristol.co.uk
www.redcliffepress.co.uk

British Library Cataloguing-in-Publication Data
A catalogue record for this book is available from the British Library

Design and typesetting by Stephen Morris Communications, smc@freeuk.com
Bristol and Liverpool
Printed and bound by The Charlesworth Group, Wakefield

Contents

Publisher's note
All maps are approximate and not to scale.
At the time of publication all routes were carefully
checked and followed public rights of way.

Introduction

LIKE THE COLOUR OF YOUR EYES, AND WHETHER OR NOT YOU CAN CURL YOUR TONGUE, WALKING IS HEREDITARY. If your parents took you walking for pleasure when you were a child, then the chances are that you will relive the experience with your own children.

On the last day of October 2005, The Countryside and Rights of Way Act created a new right to walk over areas of open countryside and registered common land (although common sense restrictions still apply). We can all now enjoy vast mapped areas of land, much of which was previously off limits.

It has never been easier to go out into the countryside and enjoy the landscapes, the wildlife and the changing seasons. If you have children with you, it's important to know where you're heading, how long the walk is likely to last, if there's anywhere you can stop for refreshments and whether or not you'll be able to return to your starting point.

It's for these reasons that we've put together *24 Family Walks in and around Bristol*. We've all enjoyed walking with our parents, our children, and even our grandchildren, but we also know the experience is much more pleasurable when we know what to expect. We also appreciate that it's unreasonable to ask small children to trek across large swathes of countryside so we've included plenty of shorter walks that can easily be undertaken in an hour or so. There are walks suitable for wheelchair users too. As well as rural walks, there are several urban walks, and a few that surprised us – rural walks that can be found in very urban areas – if you know where to look. We've made sure all the walks will have some point of appeal to children, either a landmark along the way, or a challenge, or a particularly interesting and unusual history. This helps counter the question: 'But why are we going for a walk?' which invariably contains the hidden implication 'When we could be doing something more interesting instead...'

Walking with children should be a relaxing and rewarding experience. It's a chance to be really close to nature, to see rabbits, squirrels, hares, foxes, deer and all manner of birds, insects, trees, fungi and flowers in their natural environment. The walks will change all the time depending on the weather, the time of year and the time of day.

The benefits of walking are obvious. For one thing, it's about the healthiest habit you can instil in your children. Walking is excellent, natural exercise for human beings of all ages. Adults who walk briskly for just an hour and a half a week, burn up calories equivalent to 10lbs of fat over the course of a year.

It's also good for mental health. Walking stimulates a sense of wellbeing and calmness. Of course it's not a universal pick-me-up, but as anyone who walks regularly knows, it's an almost unbeatable way of relaxing and 'grounding' oneself, especially when faced with a pile of problems. If your children can find this out for themselves at an early age, they'll be able to reap the benefits for the rest of their lives. When the going gets tough, the tough put on their boots and get going.

Take your children out on your own, and you'll have the time to talk to each other without any of the usual distractions and pressures. You'll have space to play, to explore and to mess around, precious and important aspects of being part of a family. You may have certain favourite walks which are part of the annual traditions of your family. We always take a hangover-busting walk up the steep hill to Cadbury Camp in Tickenham on New Year's Day, with other families. It's something we've been doing since the children were very small, and they still look forward to this ritual with endearing and enduring enthusiasm.

Walking is free. There are no school holiday supplements. And finally, it's fun. It's the best fun you can have in daylight hours no matter how old or young you are, how fit or unfit you are. You don't need any experience, you can start right away.

There are a few tips we've picked up during the course of researching this book:

1 It sounds obvious, but do make sure that all members of the party are wearing appropriate footwear, especially in winter. The countryside around Bristol can be exceptionally wet and muddy and walking in sopping socks is no fun. Also, if you're travelling by car, it's a good idea to have spare socks and shoes in the boot just in case.

2 With children, have some kind of refreshment with you, even on the shortest walk. That way you can avoid altercations of the 'But I need a drink NOW!' variety which have spoiled many a family walk.

3 When walking, it's safest to follow designated footpaths, but anyone who walks regularly will be constantly frustrated by footpath signs disappearing between one side of a field and the other. This is partly a hangover from the grim days of the foot-and-mouth epidemic, when many farmers removed signs to help protect their animals. However it's incredibly unsettling to find yourself in the middle of nowhere and no idea where you should be going – so hopefully this this book will come in useful.

4 Don't be afraid to follow footpaths through fields of livestock, although do keep dogs on a lead. Even the best behaved and softest family pet can sometimes

turn into a monster around sheep.

5 I am not a fan of cows myself, but providing you follow the golden rule of NEVER walking between a cow and her calf, you shouldn't run into problems. If the footpath goes between cows and calves, just divert around the back of the cows, giving them a wide berth. Young cows are very inquisitive, and it's quite common for them to trot after you, especially if you have a dog with you. If this happens, don't panic. If they are worrying you, turn round to face them, make yourself as large as possible by flapping your arms, and make a loud buzzing noise, like a mosquito. This makes them back off.

6 Some of these walks include potentially dangerous features such as deep, fast-flowing rivers, cliffs and the occasional road. We've tried to be as explicit as possible in our descriptions of potential dangers, but do keep an eye on your children near water and high places.

We could go on about following the countryside code and making sure you shut all gates and not dropping litter etc but you know all that already. We just hope you enjoy reading this book as much as we enjoyed putting it together, and that it will help you make the most of your walking around the beautiful city of Bristol.

Acknowledgements

Thank you to my parents, Janet and Michael Beer who taught me to enjoy walking in the first place, to Chris, Nick and especially Mark, who took some of the pictures in this book, to Kevin, who's walked a long way with me and to Polly, who never turns down the offer of a walk. Also thanks to all my children-and-dog walking friends – we've had so many laughs and got so muddy together over the years – a huge thank you to everyone who's taken me walking and showed me new walks, and finally to John, Angela and Clara, thanks for everything, and for involving family and friends Amy, George, Joseph, Katie and the two Sophies.

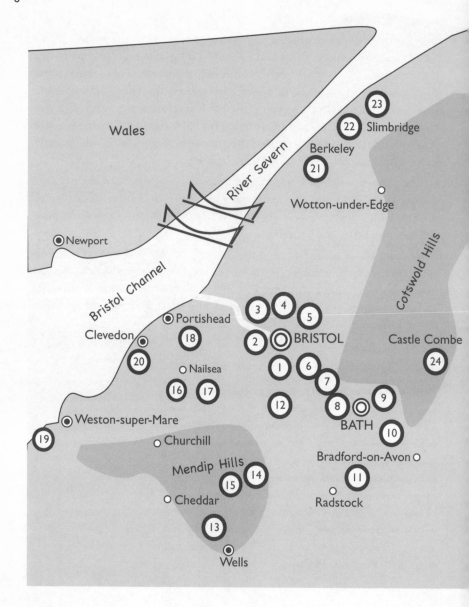

Wales

River Severn

Berkeley

21

22 Slimbridge

23

Wotton-under-Edge

Newport

Bristol Channel

Cotswold Hills

Portishead

Clevedon

18

20

Nailsea

16   17

3   4

5

2   BRISTOL

1   6

7

12

8

9

Castle Combe

24

Weston-super-Mare

Churchill

Mendip Hills

14

15

Cheddar

13

Wells

BATH

10

Bradford-on-Avon

11

Radstock

BRISTOL AND AROUND

Mervyn Peake illustration courtesy Sebastian Peake

Treasure Island |

IN SEARCH OF PIRATES REAL AND IMAGINED

GETTING THERE
From the centre of Bristol, go into Baldwin Street, right into Queen Charlotte Street, left into Crow Lane, right into Welsh Back, and try to find somewhere to park at the side of the road. Unless you're walking on a Sunday, you'll have to pay and display. Alternatively, leave the car in the NCP at the entrance to Queen Charlotte Street.

Distance: About 1 mile (1.6 km).

Walking time: Allow about 45 minutes for walking, perhaps the same again for stopping and looking at boats, caves, and other interesting things, and the same again for a refreshment stop.

Suitability: Suitable for buggies, pushchairs and wheelchairs. Some of the walk is over cobbles but it's all flat and level. This walk is suitable for everyone, and it's a pleasant walk in its own right. However, if you've read *Treasure Island*, either as part of the Great Reading Adventure, or just because it's such a good book, then you'll really enjoy this walk. Take care with roads, especially at Redcliffe Bridge.

Facilities: There's no shortage of facilities on this walk which takes in five pubs and passes by some of Bristol's best, and trendiest eateries. Apart from the pubs, you can refresh yourselves at one of the waterside snack bars, or there's always the übercool Mud Dock café/restaurant with its fine views over the water, and delicious food and drinks. Better still, stop off at the Arnolfini, and you can either eat inside the café/bar which has reopened after a fantastic designer facelift (even if you don't eat inside, go and have a look at it, it's stunning), or on a nice day sit at the bench-tables outside and watch the world go by.

BACKGROUND

WE DECIDED TO INCLUDE THE TREASURE ISLAND TRAIL in this book after hearing about the Long John Silver Trust, a charity which is campaigning to have Bristol's influence on the literary scene recognised.

As well as devising the route for the Treasure Island Trail, the Trust has also come up with the brilliant idea of bringing Robert Louis Stevenson's classic story to life, vis-à-vis a series of high quality sculptures and artworks along the way.

It's all great fun. If this ambitious scheme comes off, these sculptures would be sited sympathetically against the backdrop of Bristol's surviving historic streets and inns, prominently placed with a good view from the floating harbour, so they could also be enjoyed by passengers on the ferry-boats. There may even, in time, be a dedicated Pirate boat to enable parties of school children and people with disabilities to participate in the trail.

As both the walk and the background are inextricably linked on this occasion, we've combined the two. This walk is entirely based on information provided by Mark Steeds and the Long John Silver Trust.

If you haven't read *Treasure Island*, we promise you'll still enjoy the walk. But if you have read, or are reading, the book, then your imagination will really be able to run riot as you imagine the characters in the real-life locations which could have been the inspiration for the scenes in the story. Some of the characters were also based on real-life people who used to live in Bristol, and on this literary walk, you will literally be following in their footsteps.

The (very abridged) plot of
Treasure Island

The story of *Treasure Island* is narrated by young Jim Hawkins and starts at his parents' inn, The Admiral Benbow. A stranger called Billy Bones rents a room there and keeps warning Jim to beware of a one-legged man. Bones is visited by a terrifying blind beggar called Blind Pew who gives him the black spot – a signal of imminent death amongst pirates. Bones dies and Jim finds a map hidden in his room just before Blind Pew returns with a band of pirates looking for the map.

Jim takes the map to Squire Trelawney and Doctor Livesey who recognize it as a treasure map showing where the infamous pirate, Captain Flint, had hidden his booty. They decide to go and retrieve it and Jim joins them and their crew, lead by Captain Smollett, aboard a ship called the *Hispaniola*. The cook is a one-legged man called Long John Silver...

Jim overhears Long John Silver and other members of the crew plotting, and realizes that most of them are actually pirates!

When they reach Treasure Island, the pirates realize their plans have been discovered and attack the Captain, Squire and Doctor to try to get the map. In the meantime, Jim, who is hiding, meets Ben Gunn, an ex-pirate who has been marooned on the island for five years.

Using Ben Gunn's coracle, Jim sails out to the *Hispaniola* and cuts its mooring ropes, hoping to thwart the pirates' plans. However he is forced to board the ship when the sea gets rough, and has to kill his arch enemy, pirate Israel Hands, in order to secure the ship.

Back on the Island, Long John Silver now has the map. He persuades the other pirates not to kill Jim, and they go off in search of the treasure, only to find the treasure chest is empty...

(without giving away the ending)

1 The trail starts at the Welsh Back end of King Street and it is here that the Trust would like to site its first statue, that of Blind Pew, overlooking the Floating Harbour. As you proceed up King Street the Llandoger Trow pub is to your left, a grand, gabled building, reputed to be the most haunted place in Bristol. Even on a bright, sunny day it is possible to imagine Blind Pew, tip-tapping his way past the Llandoger Trow, along the cobbles and on to the Admiral Benbow pub. The Admiral Benbow has been absorbed into the famous Royal Naval Volunteer pub, but you still have a pretty good idea of why Stevenson would have been so inspired by such an historic and atmospheric street.

2 Now follow the signs into Queen Square. This is where Bristol's most successful privateer, Captain Woodes Rogers lived, at number 33-35 to be precise. A privateer was supposed to be licensed (have a letter of marque) that would give him the legal right to attack ships and commerce belonging to a hostile nation. Although not exactly pirates, privateers were sometimes extremely dodgy characters – a mixture of explorer and mercenary.

Members of Bristol Corporation sponsored an expedition to the South Seas in the early eighteenth century, where Captain Woodes Rogers discovered castaway Alexander Selkirk who had survived alone for four years and four months. Together, they captured a Spanish treasure ship and eventually returned to Bristol wealthy men. Selkirk became a national celebrity and inspired Daniel Defoe to write *Robinson Crusoe*. By all accounts he enjoyed his fame, and sometimes paraded around Bristol in his goatskins! It is more than likely that Selkirk was also the inspiration for *Treasure Island*'s Ben Gunn.

3 At the far side of Queen Square is the Hole in the Wall pub – this is reputed to be the Spy-Glass Inn of *Treasure Island* fame and this is where the Long John Silver Trust would like to place a statue commemorating Stevenson's greatest creation, the anti-hero Long John Silver. The pub most closely follows the description laid down in *Treasure Island* and actually has a 'spy-hole' feature of its own.

In the book Long John Silver starts off as landlord of the Spy-Glass. The Trust would like to see him portrayed looking out towards Redcliffe. This would be doubly significant as Bristol's most infamous real-life pirate, Blackbeard, was born there.

[If you look to your left along Welsh Back halfway towards Blind Pew, the Trust would like to site a group sculpture (funds permitting) of Squire Trelawney, Captain Smollett and Dr Livesey poring over papers and planning their voyage – exactly as Woodes Rogers did in 1708 when fitting out the *Duke and Duchess* here for his epic voyage.]

4 From the Hole in the Wall, cross the road, over Redcliffe Bridge and then bear right down into Redcliffe Wharf. The Trust would like to put up a statue to Jim Hawkins here, looking up at Long John Silver on the opposite side of the river whilst leaning against some apple barrels.

This is another vital aspect of the story, as it was here (in the Trust's recreation of the story) that Hawkins overheard Long John Silver and his cut-throats plotting and planning. If some of the modern-day barrels were hollow, children

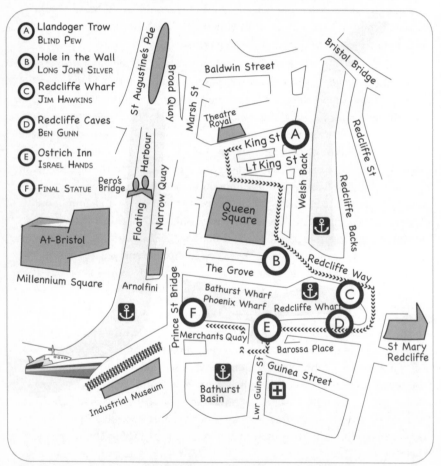

could hide in them and eavesdrop on the adults around the statue.

There's a long ramp leading up to the road from the Wharf. This is the old donkey ramp, used to move cargoes from the docked ships up onto the road. At the bottom of the ramp, is the entrance to Redcliffe caves. It's here that the Trust would like to put an artwork to Ben Gunn, whose cave plays such an essential part in the story of *Treasure Island*.

5 A little further along the quayside, you'll reach the Bathurst Basin, and at the side of this harbour within a harbour, you'll find another famous Bristol inn, the Ostrich. Here the Trust would like to erect a ship's mast and portray Israel Hands either falling to his death or pursuing Jim with his knife in his mouth.

In real life, Israel Hands was Blackbeard's navigator, and he was far luckier than his fictional counterpart. Just before Blackbeard's ship (a consort to the famous *Queen Anne's Revenge*) entered a fatal battle with the Royal Navy, Hands and Blackbeard fought and he had to go ashore to recover from his wounds, narrowly avoiding being captured, imprisoned, and almost certainly condemned to death.

(Immediately after the Ostrich, a small road goes up to the left. This is Guinea Street, and a few hundred yards up is yet another pub, this one called the Golden Guinea, another reminder of Bristol's links with pirates, privateers and the dreaded slave trade. Golden guineas were the most desirable treasure of the time – even more coveted than pieces of eight.)

6 Cross the Bathurst Basin via the blue bridge and carry on along the floating harbour, and just before you reach Prince Street Bridge, you'll reach the spot where the Trust would like to place the final sculpture, depicting one of the survivors of the quest for the treasure dragging a treasure chest behind him.

7 If you cross the bridge, you'll find yourself conveniently right at the entrance to the Arnolfini's café/bar. Alternatively, you could stay on the same side of the river and explore the Industrial Museum or walk on down to where the *Matthew* and the ss *Great Britain* are moored.

THE LONG JOHN SILVER TRUST
Would you like to see statues and artworks depicting characters and events from *Treasure Island* along the Trail?
Do you have any further ideas? If you'd like to support the Long John Silver Trust's campaign contact Mark Steeds on: 01454 238217 or by email:
mark@beaufortarms.com. If you'd like any more information visit the website at:
www.longjohnsilvertrust.co.uk
Further reading: the *Bristol Treasure Island Trail*, Broadcast Books.

Leigh Woods

2

BATS, BIRDS AND RARE PLANTS

GETTING THERE
Cross the Clifton Suspension Bridge from Clifton and take the first right into North Road. You'll see the parking spaces at the side of the woods on your right. Or, North Road can be reached from the A369, Abbots Leigh/Rownham Hill road.

Distance: Depending on whether you add on the marked purple route, either $3/4$ mile (1.2km) or 2 miles (3.2km).

Walking time: 1–2 hours.

Suitability: Part of route suitable for buggies, pushchairs or wheelchairs. At the North Road entrance to Leigh Woods there is a map which shows you how to access dedicated trails that are well laid out and marked and would be suitable for wheelchair users and pushchairs.

Terrain: The walk described here is fairly easy going with no particularly steep areas, but the paths can get muddy here and there.

If you want to walk down Nightingale Valley to the path that runs beside the River Avon, be aware that that path is steep, rocky, narrow and downright difficult in places. Also, it is the only path up and down to the river, unless you want a really long walk along the Avon to the next available footpath. From the river, don't try and find your way back up the side of the gorge along unmarked trails, it's very steep and dangerous.

Dogs: Dogs will enjoy this walk and can run free.

Parking: There is plenty of car parking along North Road.

Refreshments: Usually an ice-cream van parked on the other side of the Clifton Suspension Bridge. Alternatively, Clifton Village has places to eat and drink.

Toilets: Public toilets on the other side of the Clifton Suspension Bridge.

Warning! The Avon Gorge is steep and high, children and dogs should be kept away from the cliff edge.

PEOPLE HAVE BEEN WALKING IN LEIGH WOODS FOR THOUSANDS OF YEARS and the landscape in the woods themselves probably hasn't changed much at all. Because of the unique, relatively unmolested environment, the woods are home to some of Britain's rarest trees and plants, and are a haven for wildlife.

Nowadays, people use the Suspension Bridge, or the Cumberland Basin to cross the River Avon. Before these crossings were built, there was the Rownham ferry. Rolinda Sharples painted a wonderful scene in 1820 of the ferry packed with passengers, probably on their way to the Long Ashton tea-gardens which were then a popular excursion for Bristolians. This painting and other wonderful views of the Gorge are included in a book called *From Bristol to the Sea* by Francis Greenacre, and many of the paintings can be seen in Bristol Art Gallery. But, believe it or not, for centuries people would actually walk across the river. More or less exactly underneath the Suspension Bridge, there used to be a ford which people used to cross the river at low tide. Beneath the mud at the bottom of the river, there is rock, which served as a sort of road across the river.

For centuries, ancient people would walk down the track which is now Bridge Valley Road, wade across the river, and walk back up the other side of the gorge along the footpath which still leads down to the river through Nightingale Valley, running parallel with North Road.

Of course, when big ships started using the docks at Bristol, the ford became a problem – they kept scraping their bottoms on the rock, so in 1894 it was blown up.

For the ancient people who used to live in this neck of the woods, the top of the cliffs overlooking the gorge, and the crossing point, were perfect spots from which to defend their territory, so sensibly they built camps on either side of the river. This walk encompasses the Iron-Age hill fort at Stokeleigh Camp, one of three such forts on the Avon Gorge. It's not particularly obvious, but you can still see much of the earthworks left from what was once a large, triangular-shaped camp.

Stokeleigh Camp dates back to around 350 BC but people were living and hunting in the woods long before that. Neolithic arrow heads and axe heads have been found in the forests. If it weren't for the noise from the traffic on the Portway, which it's impossible to escape on this walk, then it would be easy to imagine yourself back in prehistoric times.

There are possibly thousands of squirrels in the woods. In autumn the canopies of the trees rustle and jump as the nut-hunting and gathering gets into full swing. It's also a good spot for jackdaws, which nest in the buttress of the Suspension Bridge. Jackdaws are members of the crow family. You can recognise them by the silver hood at the back of their heads and their white eyes. Because the gorge acts like a funnel for the wind, it provides updrafts on warm days which are ideal soaring conditions for birds of prey including peregrine falcons, buzzards, goshawks, sparrowhawks, and red kites.

Local mythology has it that at high tide you might spot a roe deer swimming across the river. Sadly, we've never met anyone who's actually seen it.

The Avon Gorge is a site of Special Scientific Interest. It's also home to greater and lesser horseshoe bats which roost in the little caves on either side of the river in the winter. These bats live only in South-West England and are an endangered species. Other kinds of bats hunt in the gorge too.

Because the gorge has its own microclimate, it is home to some of Britain's rarest plants. It is believed that the seeds which grew into the ancestors of the plants there today were actually brought into the gorge during the last ice age. Amongst the rare trees are the Bristol Whitebeam and the Wilmotts's Whitebeam, both unique to the gorge. If you're the sort of family who knows your onions, then you might also be able to spot the Bristol onion, or even the Autumn Squill!

In Victorian times, Nightingale Valley was very popular with artists, who would visit the woods to sketch and paint. It's still popular with creative people today, thanks to the dramatic views, the abundance of wildlife, and the unique atmosphere.

THE WALK LEIGH WOODS

1 Go through the gate at North Road. The path to your right leads down to the gorge through Nightingale Valley. The path to your left takes you on a ramble through the woods towards Avon Gorge Nature Reserve. Instead, take the path directly in front of you. It leads into an open, grassed area. On your left is a very attractive group of Arts and Craft houses. At the other side of the open area are two clear paths. Take the right-hand path through the trees.

2 This path leads you directly to Stokeleigh Camp. On the way you will enjoy some of the most spectacular views over the Suspension Bridge and the Gorge. See what you can pick out on the other side of the Gorge. In the cliff face opposite is the look-out where the Giant's Cave opens onto the cliff face. Among the buildings behind, you should be able to see the copper tower of the Clifton College chapel. To the left, are disused quarries. If they hadn't put a stop to quarrying in the nineteenth century, the gorge wouldn't be as spectacular or Romantic as it is. (It used to be really dramatic before the quarrying started.)

3 From here, follow the footpath round to the right. If this is a long enough walk for you, turn left by the pond just beyond the earthworks, you'll end up back in the open area where you started. But before you do, take a good look at the earthworks. With the approval of English Heritage, the trees here have been felled, and you can now now clearly see the distinctive ramparts and ditches.

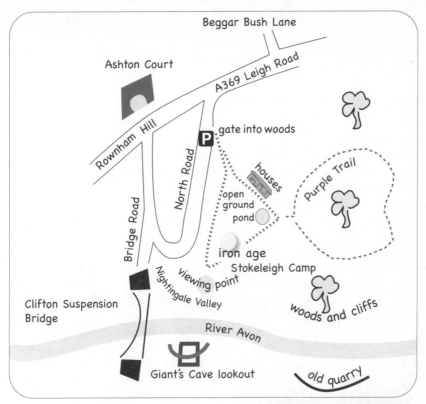

Map showing Ashton Court, A369 Leigh Road, Beggar Bush Lane, Rownham Hill, North Road, Bridge Road, P (gate into woods), houses, Purple Trail, open ground, pond, iron age Stokeleigh Camp, viewing point, Nightingale Valley, Clifton Suspension Bridge, River Avon, Giant's Cave lookout, woods and cliffs, old quarry.

These were built to enclose the interior of the hill fort, protecting the inhabitants from attacks by rival tribes in the area.

4 If you want to make the walk a little longer, follow the path straight ahead. You've now connected with the designated 1$\frac{1}{2}$ miles (2.5km) Purple Trail. If you keep following the arrows you will eventually end up back at the open area.

5 This extended trail takes you through the woods, but there are very few views or glimpses of the gorge. There are, however, some sculptures to look out for en route and the marker posts are decorated with flora and fauna you can spot along the way.

Kings Weston Down
and Penpole Woods   3

A GRAND HOUSE AND NATURE RESERVE

Distance: $2^1/_2$ miles (4 km).

Walking time: $1^1/_2$ hours.

Suitability: The walk is not suitable for wheelchairs – but there are paths around Kings Weston House which are easily accessible and fine for wheelchair users.

Terrain: This is a good, easy walk with no steep climbs or descents, but there can be some muddy patches. Even small children should manage this walk without any trouble. It's ideal for a Sunday afternoon outing for all the family – from grannies to the little ones.

Dogs: A perfect walk for dogs.

Parking: Woodland car park.

Refreshments: The vaulted tea shop at Kings Weston House is open every day of the year except Christmas Day from 10am until 4pm. There's a very good selection of meals, or you can just have a cup of tea and a snack. The tea shop is licensed so adults can enjoy wine or beer with their meal. There's also a very pleasant outdoor area to relax on warm days. Alternatively, you could enjoy a pre-booked Sunday lunch in the dining room at Kings Weston House before or after your walk.

Tel: 0117 938 2299 or visit www.kingswestonhouse.co.uk

Toilets: There are toilets and baby changing facilities for customeris of the tea shop and restaurant.

GETTING THERE

From the Portway, turn into Sylvan Way then left at the traffic lights into Shirehampton Road. Drive on following signs to Blaise Castle and Kings Weston House. Pass under green footbridge until eventually you turn left into Kings Weston Lane, following the signs for Kings Weston House. Turn left into the drive for Kings Weston House and then immediately left into the Woodland Car Park. Or if you're coming from the direction of Westbury-on-Trym, go down Kings Weston Road (B4057), turning right into Kings Weston Lane.

KINGS WESTON DOWN IS ACTUALLY PART OF THE BLAISE CASTLE ESTATE, although this feels like a completely different part of Bristol. It is possible to walk from Kings Weston House to Blaise Castle House Museum without ever crossing a road – and if you have lots of energy and lots of time this would be a very enjoyable ramble.

However, as Kings Weston Down is roughly a mile long, and can be reached from the Shirehampton and Westbury-on-Trym sides, it's a good family walk in its own right with a completely different ambience to the Blaise Castle walk.

The walk starts and finishes in the grounds of Kings Weston House, a very fine, grand villa which, when it was built around 1710, would have enjoyed fabulous views across the Bristol Channel. The views are still there, but so are Avonmouth, the M5, and the long, straggling line of industrial buildings and chimneys that border the Bristol side of the Severn Estuary.

The house as it stands today was designed by Sir John Vanbrugh for Edward Southall, but there was a big house on the site before this one. William III stayed at Kings Weston in 1690. Now the house is a venue for events and weddings and boasts a fantastic portrait gallery (well worth popping in for a look if the house is open) and a unique, hanging staircase in the Great Hall.

Not all that long ago, this was the headquarters of the Avon and Somerset police – before they moved into their purpose-built premises outside Portishead. During the war, it was an army camp. You can still see concrete slabs all over the place – these are all that remain of scores of Nissen huts where the soldiers used to live. When the war finished, the Nissen huts were used to house a second army – this one consisting of hundreds of mainly Irish labourers brought in to build the extended Brabazon runway at Filton.

The Brabazon was a gigantic plane built by the Bristol Aeroplane Company to fly wealthy passengers between England and America.

When the Brabazon was finished in 1949, it was bigger by 10 metres than a Boeing 747 and the most technologically advanced aircraft in the world. Sadly, it proved completely impractical and it never flew commercially.

1 From the car park, follow the sign to the left marked 'Reception'. This brings you out on to a good, wide path. Look to your right, and you'll see the grand façade of Kings Weston House in front of you. That's where you'd go to visit the tea shop. However, to reach Kings Weston Down, you need to turn left, and walk between the avenue of trees to the folly at the top. You can see that people living in the big house would have had a wonderful view of the folly. At one point, statues would have stood in the alcoves of this strange little building (the gargoyles on the vases on top are really unusual). It's a good place for a photo opportunity of children pretending to be statues.

2 Now cut through the path at the right-hand side of the building, down the steps, and bear left over the metal bridge which crosses the road. Once on the other side, carry on straight ahead and into Kings Weston Down. The views from this point are lovely in winter – when the leaves are on the trees it's hard to see much, but the River Avon is visible from here.

3 Follow the path up onto the Down, and, once you've passed the fenced-off old quarry (now a wildlife haven) and the TV mast on your right, you have a mile of

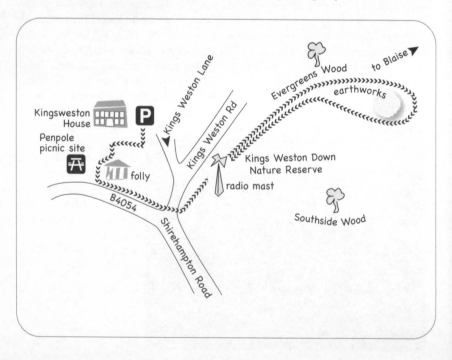

unadulterated playground in front of you. There's woodland on either side of the Down which is a magnet for birds and butterflies. The wide Down is a perfect spot for kite-flying or just running around.

It's an easy walk, whether brisk or the ambling sort. At the far end, you'll find the grassed-over remains of an iron age fort. The earliest evidence of human life found on the hill were flints used by Neolithic farmers some 5,000 years ago. After that, stone-age settlers came, and you can still make out the shape of their burial mounds. The embankment of the later, iron age fort is clearly visible, as are the remains of what is believed to be an old Roman road dissecting the Down a little further back.

4 This is as far as you can go without heading downhill towards Blaise Castle. So at this point, we recommend turning round and retracing your steps to Kings Weston House for some well earned refreshments.

Penpole Woods

From the same starting point, there is a second, equally attractive but shorter walk. This time, from the car park, turn right and walk down to Kings Weston House. Follow the path to the left of the building, and then, with your back to the house, follow the fence in a straight line, with the huge, grassy area to your left. There are great views across the Channel to your right but there is, unfortunately, noise from the M5.

The path continues under some trees and carries on into Penpole woods. It's a short, but beautiful walk, with some huge, dramatic trees. At the end is Penpole Point where you can stop and admire the views over Avonmouth. It's one of those walks where the travelling is better than the arriving but one that's well worth doing, and truly lovely on a sunny day.

Blaise Castle

4

A FAIRYTALE LANDSCAPE AND A GREAT PLAYGROUND

Distance: About 2¹/₂ miles (4km).

Walking time: 1–2 hours (depending how much time is spent paddling/playing en route).

Suitability: Not suitable for buggies, push-chairs or wheelchairs.

Terrain: This walk isn't too demanding and is suitable for children aged about four upwards. Not suitable for pushchairs or wheelchair users.

Facilities: The Blaise Castle Estate has wonder-ful, Heritage Lottery-funded facilities.

Parking: Free, public car park at the entrance to the grounds.

Refreshments: Café (and there's usually an ice-cream van in the car park too).

Toilets: Public toilets.

There are excellent adventure playgrounds to suit children of different age groups as well as

GETTING THERE

From the A4018 (accessed either from M5 Junction 17 or from Westbury-on-Trym) take the B4057 (Crow Lane) at the roundabout (sign-posted Blaise Castle). Follow the road through the one-way system into the B4057 Kings Weston Road.
The entrance to the Blaise Castle Estate car park is several hundred metres further than the House, on the left-hand side.

acres of green space in which to walk the dog or enjoy a picnic. The walk takes you straight past Blaise Castle Museum and it's well worth having a quick look at the fairytale cottages in Blaise Hamlet while you're in the area.

BLAISE CASTLE ESTATE, although relatively close to the centre of Bristol, is 650-acres of woodland, castle, cottages, rivers and incredibly dramatic scenery.

The Castle itself is actually a folly, built on the site of St Blaise's Chapel, which used to stand on the hill overlooking the gorge on one side, and the gentler slopes of Henbury on the other, and which was originally a Roman camp. The gothic Castle was built in 1766 and was used by its owners as a summer house. It is usually open on Sundays during the summer and you can go inside for free.

The main house, designed by Bristol architect William Paty, was built of Bath stone in 1796 and is now a fascinating museum of everyday life. Entry is free and exhibits include a collection of toys and games, and landscape designer Humphry Repton's original red book, which shows drawings and paintings of the grounds. Behind the house is a thatched dairy designed by John Nash.

Blaise Castle Hamlet was designed by Nash under instruction from John Harford, the wealthy merchant who owned Blaise House. He wanted to provide homes for his retired staff, and came up with the idea of a small hamlet of storybook appearance, and that's exactly what he got. Blaise Hamlet is an incredibly sweet collection of nine little cottages, each different, built around a village green complete with weather vane and water pump. There are benches outside each house where the retired servants could sit and chat of an evening in the shade of the abundant fruit trees. It really is the nearest thing you can get to being inside a fairy tale without watching *Shrek*. The cottages belong to the National Trust and are still inhabited, though not by elderly servants.

The Hamlet is an easy walk from the Estate car park (although take care crossing the very fast Kings Weston Road). Turn right out of the car park, then take the first left. The Hamlet can be reached via a signed gate in the wall.

1 From the car park, take the path past the new visitor centre and follow it past the adventure playgrounds (note: you will probably have to stop here while the children have a go on the equipment), keeping right as it curves downhill past the main house.

2 To your left, you'll see the stream which will eventually grow into the River Trym. Follow the path down to the recently restored Mill. This is Stratford Mill and it wasn't originally sited here but was moved to its current location in the 1960s to preserve it for future generations.

3 Cross over the little bridge and either take the left-hand path which zigzags uphill steeply to a unique little 'Hansel and Gretel' style cottage made entirely of

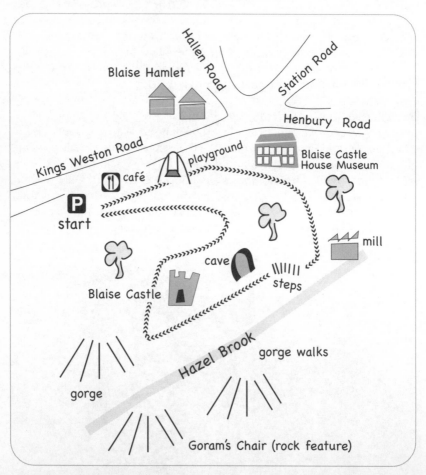

wood (once there, it's best to turn back unless you feel like a much longer walk along the Rhododendron Path) or follow the lower, flatter path alongside the stream. A huge restoration project has resulted in some lovely little bridges and the wildlife is pretty and diverse at any time of year. Weather permitting, children and dogs generally enjoy paddling in the shallow parts of the stream.

4 With the water on your right, keep going until you reach a second bridge, cross over, and head back along the gorge with the water again on your right.

If you look up, you'll see Lover's Leap, the dramatic precipice which towers above the gorge. Also along the gorge, look out for the giant Goram's armchair – an immense limestone rock formation.

5 Keep going until you reach some steps to your left. Climb these steps and follow the path up the side of the gorge. Halfway up there's a cave built into the rockface and see if you can spot Goram's enormous footprint – it's quite clear in the rock at the side of the path.

The views become more spectacular as the path ascends, and there's a good, fenced lookout point towards the top where you can gaze across the gorge over the valley towards Shirehampton. A little further up, the path opens out into green space at the top of the hill and you'll see Blaise Castle in front of you.

6 Once you've finished exploring/picnicking, there are several paths down. Perhaps the most straightforward is the path marked by three large fir trees, almost diagonally opposite the spot where you first saw the Castle. This leads back down to the grassy area between the car park and the house via a series of slopes and steps.

If you feel like refreshment after all that exertion, now's the time to visit the café.

Snuff Mills 5

A PRETTY PARK AND A PADDLE

Distance: About $1^3/_4$ miles (3 km).

Walking time: 2 hours.

Suitability: Suitable for buggies, pushchairs or wheelchairs for part of the way (but stick to major paths).

Terrain: Perfect for children of all ages. You can vary the route depending on age and ability of the children.

Dogs: A very good walk for well-behaved dogs.

Parking: Car park at the Snuff Mills entrance to the walk.

Refreshments: Tea rooms are open in summer. En route, there are lots of good places for picnics, at plenty of benches and viewing points.

Toilets: In Snuff Mills car park and at the playground in Oldbury Court Estate.

GETTING THERE

Take the M32 out of Bristol and leave at the IKEA junction (J2). Stay in the middle lane off the slip road and cross straight over to Stapleton Road which goes uphill beside the M32, crosses beneath it, and then becomes Bell Hill and Park Road. At the mini roundabout, turn right into Broom Hill, and then left into River View. The car park is at the end of this very pretty little road.

IF YOU WANTED, YOU COULD FOLLOW THE COURSE OF THE RIVER FROME all the way from the Centre of Bristol to the Cotswold Hills for 18 miles, although the river has been culverted for some of that way where it disappears under the M32.

There are several sections of the Frome Walkway in Bristol which are very pleasant for families; we've chosen this one because it has some historical interest, because it's very pleasant for adults as well as children, and because there's a really good playground in the Oldbury Court Estate.

The name 'Frome' comes from the Anglo-Saxon word 'Frum' which means vigorous. It is precisely because the river is so lively that it was a powerful force at the beginning of the industrial era in the south west. A number of mills were built alongside the river including those at Snuff Mills where the walk begins.

The remains of the old mill have been preserved at the start of the walk and there are boards detailing the history of the area. The famous Pennant stone, which was used to build everything from the cottages at the entrance to the Snuff Mills car park to the Bush tea warehouse (now the famous Arnolfini gallery) was all quarried from this area.

For more than 600 years the water from the Frome powered the water wheels which worked the machinery in the mill. It is unlikely that snuff was ever actually ground in the old mill, it was more likely that that job took place a little way upstream in the old Witherly Mill where the footbridge now stands. This mill was bought by HO Wills in 1805 and snuff was ground there for several decades after that. It is from the Witherly Mill that the legend of Snuffy Jack – an old chap who was always covered in the stuff – originated.

Snuff is dried, ground tobacco which is sniffed, a habit which was very popular and fashionable in the eighteenth and nineteenth centuries. It was also scented with different oils. It is a well documented fact that much of Bristol's fortune, and certainly the great University, were built with the wealth accumulated by the Wills family from the production and sale of tobacco products. The snuff connection is far less famous than that of the cigarettes!

This walk starts at Snuff Mills and carries on into Oldbury Court Estate, the site of an old Royal Hunting Lodge. The house no longer exists, but the site is still known as 'Vassalls' after the last family who lived there. The Estate was designed by Humphry Repton (who also designed Blaise Castle Estate) and is still a delight today, with many old ornamental trees, landscaped lawns, and delightful viewpoints dotted all over.

1 From the car park, walk past the remains of the old mill alongside the river, with the river to your right. In the last mill building, you can see, half buried, a double egg-ended boiler which was installed in 1850 to power a 12-horse power steam engine. It is the only one of its kind still in its original location anywhere in the country.

2 Walk past the picnic area, and cross the footbridge over the river. It's a prettier, gentler river than the Avon at the same distance from the centre, and the path now leads you into a very beautiful valley. Simply follow the path beside the river past several attractive weirs until you reach a point where the river separates into two sections around an island, and is joined by a stream tumbling downhill from the right-hand side.

This is a very popular spot for families. The stream is shallow, and each time we have visited, the children have insisted on paddling – even in winter. They also enjoy following it uphill. It's popular with dogs, too. On a Sunday morning, you'll pass families with dogs of all breeds, colours and sizes – more than you're ever likely to see, outside Crufts. We even saw a man walking his ferret.

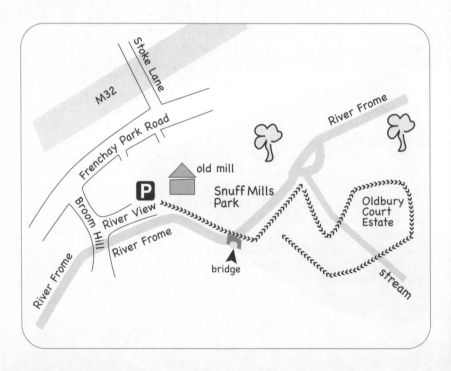

3 It's really up to you where you go from this point. The path continues beside the Frome for some time, although eventually it becomes impossible to access for wheelchairs and pushchairs but there are some pleasant picnic spots further along.

4 If you have promised children a visit to the park, take the tarmac path that goes up beside the stream, and carry along this path uphill all the way to the top. Here you can turn left into Oldbury Court Estate with its lovely open areas, its ancient trees, and beautiful views, or right into an excellent children's play area. There's usually an ice cream van in attendance, and there are plenty of benches for the adults.

5 When you finally manage to tear the children away from the play equipment, you can loop back down to the river via a second path (only this one does involve negotiating steps at the bottom), or go back the way you came up.

This is a really lovely walk but it is little known beyond the immediate area. It is so accessible that there's really no reason not to explore.

Eastwood Farm Brislington

BY THE BANKS OF THE AVON

6

Distance: About 1$^1/_2$ miles (2.5km).
Walking time: 1 hour.
Suitability: Not suitable for buggies, pushchairs or wheelchairs.
Terrain: This is a relatively easy walk with no really steep climbs or descents, but there are some muddy patches. There are benches en route where you can sit down and admire the views.
Dogs: Need to be kept away from wildlife and the river's edge.
Parking: On-street parking.
Refreshments: Beese's Tea Gardens are open from Easter to September.
Toilets: For customers of Beese's Tea Gardens.

GETTING THERE

Road: Take the Bath Road out of Bristol. At the bottom of Brislington Hill, turn left into Church Hill, don't follow it round to the right but carry on into School Road which then becomes Birchwood Road. Turn right into Eastwood Road and park at the side of the road close to the playground on the left.

Road and ferry: Beese's tea gardens operate a ferry service across the Avon on Saturdays and Sundays during the summer months. You'll have to approach from the Hanham side of the river and reach the ferry via Conham Road and Conham River Park.

By boat: On a summer weekend or bank holiday take the *Bristol Packet* from the City Centre up to Beese's tea gardens, stop off, enjoy the walk, and return by boat to Bristol. The *Bristol Packet* operates a weekend and bank holiday service to the tea gardens during the summer. www.bristolpacket.co.uk
Tel: 0117 926 8157

BACKGROUND

THIS IS ONE OF THOSE WONDERFUL SECRET WALKS that you'd never discover by accident (unless you are actually live in Wyndham Crescent or Eastwood Road) and it's quite exciting to find this beautiful, dramatic, riverside walk tucked away behind a Bristol housing estate.

If you're starting from the Brislington side of the river, parking can be a bit of a problem so we'd recommend taking the ferry option if possible. The boat ride from the city centre is truly lovely and a treat that will be enjoyed by children and adults alike.

You don't have to take refreshments at Beese's tea gardens, although you'll be continuing an historic tradition if you do. Beese's was opened in 1846 and almost immediately established itself as a popular watering hole for boat-trippers and people arriving by ferry from St George.

Apparently, this particular stretch of river also used to be popular with children because there was always a good chance of seeing a drowned corpse being pulled from the water here. You'll be relieved to know that that's highly unlikely to happen today, although the speed at which the chocolate-coloured water flows is dramatic and you will want to hang on to the hands of lively toddlers. Ducks who sit on the water and go with the flow float past at a fantastic rate of knots!

This is a popular stretch of river for rowing clubs and scullers, and there can often be river traffic jams on a fine Sunday morning!

There are some equally lovely walks on the other side of the river. Opposite Beese's, there's the site of an eight-eenth century copper works and an old sewer works at Conham river park which is now a wildlife haven. The old towpath on that side of the river is part of the River Avon Trail and popular with walkers and cyclists of all ages.

1 This is a circular walk, so join at any point but we're assuming a starting point at Beese's. If you haven't arrived by ferry, the tea gardens are reached from the Eastwood Farm path by walking uphill along a gravel path, through a stile and via the garden entrance. Leave the gardens this way to begin the walk.

2 Follow the path beside the river, keeping the river to your left. In front of you, there's a wildlife lake which is home to a myriad of birds, insects and plants and this is a great place to find herons. (Remember, if you see a heron and bow to it, you'll have good luck for a year – according to the old tradition!)

3 Now you'll find yourself in a beautiful, tree-covered gorge, with great views across the river.

This walk circles the 65-acre Eastwood Farm Nature Reserve which is managed by Bristol City Council with the support of the Countryside Agency as a place of nature conservation. Depending on the time of year you walk, you and your

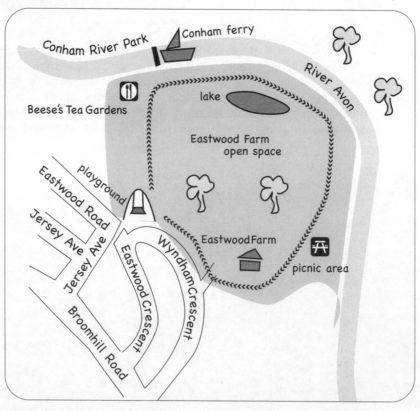

children should be able to spot dozens of varieties of birds, dragonflies, butterflies, flowers, berries, seeds and so on. This is also one of the few places in central Bristol where there's a very good chance of seeing the blue flash of a kingfisher.

The banks of the Avon are also popular with fisherfolk who are probably hoping to catch carp. In the summer months, you can spot shoals of smaller fish, such as dace, feeding near the surface of the water. The Avon is also home to chubb, trout, tench, roach, pike, perch and eels!

4 Cross a stream feeding the river via a wooden bridge, and keep going for almost as far as you can alongside the river. Eventually, you'll see a well marked path leading away to the right. If you take the wooden steps to the left of this path, you'll come to a small, but pretty picnic area with a bench. Alternatively, follow the path uphill. There are fields to your left and woods to your right.

5 At the top of the hill, the path curves round to the right up wooden steps. Turn left, cross the road that leads to Eastwood Farm and follow the path to the right off the road. The flats and houses of Wyndham Crescent skirt the woods at this point.

6 There's an exit to the playground and to Eastwood Road and the far corner of the woods (this is where you start the walk if travelling by car). The playground is not in the best condition, and definitely not worth a diversion for investigation. Instead, (unless you started the walk here) follow the path back down through the woods and after ten minutes or so you'll see Beese's tea gardens again away down to your left.

Bristol to Bath Railway Path

STEAM TRAINS AND RIVER BANK

Distance: As long as you like. The distance covered here is about $1^1/_2$ miles (2km) each way.

Walking time: $1^1/_2$ hours.

Suitability: A very good walk for buggies, pushchairs and wheelchairs.

Terrain: Perfect for just about anyone of any ability. This is a flat, straight, well surfaced walk and you can go for as short or as long a walk as time and legs allow. It's also ideal for children (and adults) who want to travel by bicycle.

Dogs: Dogs are allowed along the railway path, but it's not ideal for them and there is a danger of collision with cyclists.

Parking: Car park at Bitton station.

Refreshments: Café at Bitton station.

Toilets: At Bitton station.

This walk goes as far as the Riverside Picnic Area, which is a lovely place to stop. There's also a really good pub off the A4175 called the Lock Keeper's which does food and has lots of seating inside and out.

GETTING THERE

From Bristol, take the A4 towards Bath out of Brislington. At the Hicks Gate roundabout, turn right (towards Keynsham) and follow the A4175 through Keynsham, past the Cadbury's chocolate factory to Willsbridge. Turn right on to the Bath Road, left into Cherry Garden Road and left again into Pines Road which takes you to Bitton station car park.

BACKGROUND

THE BRISTOL AND BATH RAILWAY PATH is 13 miles (21km) long and follows the route of the old Midland Railway. This section of the route actually runs alongside the only working part of the railway, now called the Avon Valley Railway which currently starts and ends at Bitton Station.

The station is something of a museum piece. It's been beautifully looked after, and what seem like scores of enthusiasts are always on hand to maintain and drive the genuine, old-fashioned steam trains. They have also managed to re-lay some three miles (5km) of track, and have restored several engines and many carriages.

The section of the railway line between Mangotsfield and Bitton is one of the oldest. It was opened in 1835 and was used for transporting coal from the mines at Kingswood to Bristol docks. In the beginning, horses used to pull the wagons. Soon the line was converted to use by steam trains, and it became part of the national rail network with an extra section linking Bitton to Bath in 1869. This railway line remained in use until it fell victim to Dr Beeching's axe in the late Sixties. It's largely thanks to Bristol-based Sustrans (the charity which campaigns for sustainable forms of transport) and a band of dedicated volunteers that we are able to walk the path today.

The railway track goes as far north as Oldland Common, and Avon Valley Railway is now concentrating on restoring it southwards, back towards Bristol. It's not a cheap process. It costs around £100,000 per mile of track.

Because the story of Avon Valley Railway resembles that of the Phoenix rising from the ashes, you may notice that some of the trains carry the name 'Midland Phoenix'.

You could, of course, simply go for a ride on a train (you can even have your birthday party on one of the Avon Valley trains), but it's very nice to walk – or cycle – along the path and watch the trains go by. That way, you get to smell the smoke too!

As well as being a convenient and attractive way to travel between Bristol and Bath without ever meeting a car, the path is an important corridor for wildlife. It's well worth doing the whole walk, but not all sections are as attractive, or interesting as others. We picked out this one for the purposes of the book because of the interest provided by Avon Valley Railway, and because the picnic spot makes a good point for which to aim.

You can not reach the Avon Riverside Picnic Area by road – it is only accessible from the railway path or from the river itself (there is a landing area), all of which adds to the sense of fun and occasion. In 2004, Avon Valley Railway opened a new station – complete with platform, called Avon Riverside. This means you could catch the train one (or both) ways if you feel it is too far to walk to the picnic area.

1 Cross the railway line between Bitton Station and the car park and almost at once you're out in the countryside following a long, straight path towards Bath. There are lovely views to both sides of the Avon Valley and plenty for nature lovers to enjoy. You will almost certainly see volunteers working on the railway beside you, and at the weekends you'd be unlucky if you weren't passed by a steam train at least once.

2 To the left, you can see Bitton church and the rising ground of Upton Cheyney, to the right is Avon Valley, with the famous Country Park sweeping along the far side of the river. You can work out where the river lies from the line of trees which border it.

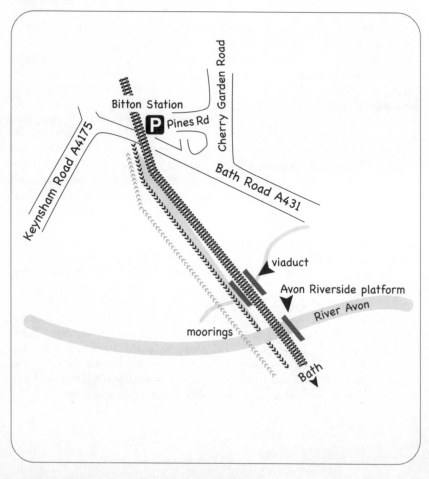

3 After about a mile and a half you reach the place where the railway path crosses the Avon – you'll recognise it by the new Avon Riverside railway platform at the side of the path.

4 There's a path down to the river, with mooring for boats, which is a truly lovely place to stop and relax.

5 After that, you could either carry on further, or turn round and amble back to Bitton station.

Swineford to Kelston Round Hill 8

A WALK WITH LEGENDS AND AN ANCIENT HILL FORT

Distance: About 3½ miles (5.6 km).

Walking time: 2–3 hours.

Suitability: Not suitable for buggies, pushchairs or wheelchairs.

Terrain: This is a really good legstretcher of a walk, with a steady climb up from Swineford to a high point of 230 metres above sea level at Prospect Stile overlooking Kelston Round Hill which is slightly lower at 218 metres. It's too far for very small children, but a great day out for older ones, taking in a good long stretch of the Cotswold Way (a designated national trail) and some of the best countryside between Bristol and Bath.

GETTING THERE

From Bristol, head for Bitton and take the A371, the north route into Bath. Swineford picnic area is signposted to the left. If you pass the Swan Inn you've gone too far.

Dogs: This is a good walk for dogs but you'll need to keep them on a lead in fields with livestock.

Parking: There's a free car park at the start of the walk at Swineford Picnic Area. As its name suggests, it's a very good place for a picnic, well away from the main road and in a pretty, quiet location with bench-tables and a little stream babbling by.

Refreshments: There are a couple of good pubs close by, in particular the Swan Inn which is right by the picnic area. It's an attractive, family-friendly place serving good food. Up Brewery Lane you'll find the pretty village of Upton Cheney, which has an excellent pub, the Upton Inn. Alternatively, Bath is only about five miles (8km) from Swineford.

Toilets: None.

KELSTON ROUND HILL, with its charact-eristic 'tump' of trees on top, is a landmark for people living in Bristol, Bath, and all the towns, villages and hamlets in between. The only way to reach it is by foot (you can cycle past the hill but to get right up to it you have to walk). The Cotswold Way national trail passes right beside it, and there are plenty of things to keep the family interested and involved in the walk all the way.

Swineford, at the start of the walk, is a very small village which was built up around the point where a stream, a tributary of the Avon, crossed the old Roman Road from Bath to Bristol.

One of many legends has it that this is the place where Prince Bladud, founder of Bath and father of King Lear, was cured of his leprosy. The Prince had been banned from court because of his illness and forced to look after pigs to earn his keep. The pigs also suffered from some kind of skin disease. When the Prince herded his pigs across the stream at Swineford, they were miraculously cured by the mud. He followed suit and was also cured. He went on to become King and founded Bath in 860 BC.

Just up the hill from Swineford is the picturesque hamlet of North Stoke. The word 'Stoke' usually means a 'secondary settlement' and often it has some kind of religious connotation. In this case, the Manor of North Stoke was given to Bath Abbey by the King of Mercia and it only reverted to the Crown during the dissolution of the monasteries.

St Martin's church at North Stoke is perched rather precariously on a steep part of the hill, with commanding views. If you can persuade your child-ren to detour slightly, it's worth a visit. Its records date back to 1309 and most of the early rectors were monks from Bath Abbey until the 1536 dissolution.

There's a raised, paved path up to the church. The villagers needed this in the old days when mud and rain washing down from the hill made the lane too slippery and dangerous for pedestrians. There are still two ponds for draining rain water at the steps at the entrance to the church.

Further up the hill again, there are the remains of Little Down iron age Hill Fort. You can see one of the ramp-arts still although you wouldn't notice it if you didn't know it was there.

On top of the hill, you find yourself at the far end of Bath Racecourse – the highest racecourse in England! If you're lucky enough to be walking on a race day, you may well see some horses as the path passes right past the area where they sometimes start their races. You can clearly see the stands off to your left.

1 From the Swineford Picnic Area car park, there are several marked footpaths. You need to head towards the large house at the entrance to the site. Just before you reach the house, turn left, so that you have the garden wall to your right, and the channel with the stream to your left. In front of you is a stile. Walk straight across this field to the stile on the other side, and then straight across the second field. Once you climb over this next stile, you'll find yourself on what used to be an old Roman Road.

> **Cow Alert!** Please note that during the course of this walk, you may find yourself crossing fields full of cows, some of which will probably be lying right across the track. I'm not a great fan of cows, but these cows are used to walkers and they didn't take the slightest notice of us. Do give them some berth if you have a dog with you though.

2 Follow the track uphill, past some stables until it curves round and joins the lane. You're now in the Cotswold hamlet of North Stoke. Bear left and follow the lane up the hill until you reach St Martin's church. On the way, you'll pass some beautiful houses, some of them very grand, as well as some picture-postcard pretty cottages.

3 The next bit is slightly tricky as the path is not well defined and not well marked. Keep the church on your right, and follow the lane round – it turns into a rough track. Follow the track uphill and after about 45m you'll see a stile in a gap in the hedge on your right. It's marked with a yellow arrow. Climb over the stile and follow the field to the back of the church, following the direction of the yellow arrow on a post by the wall of the church.

4 Walk through the field behind the church, gradually making your way uphill. You'll come to another post with a yellow arrow pointing you uphill. The next field is rough and there's no obvious path at all, but head for the centre of the field, and then just go straight up, heading for the highest point. If you look to your right now, you should be able to make out the rampart of the old hill fort.

5 At this point, go through a metal gate and join the Cotswold Way which is very well marked and there's no danger of wandering off the path from here on!

6 Turn right at the top and follow the Cotswold Way pointers. First you'll walk through the centre of a field and then along the edge of the next one. Continuing on, the path takes you to the white barriers which mark the side of Bath Racecourse. It's a lovely, open space and it does give you a different perspective on how far the horses have to run.

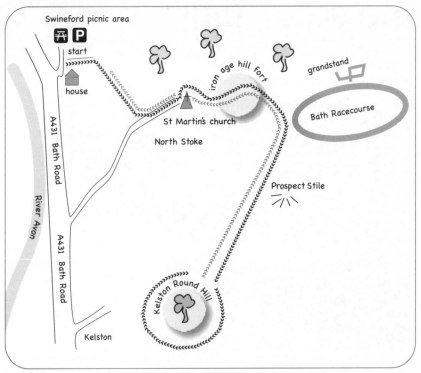

Swineford picnic area

start

house

A431 Bath Road

River Avon

A431 Bath Road

Kelston

iron age hill fort

St Martin's church

North Stoke

Prospect Stile

Kelston Round Hill

grandstand

Bath Racecourse

7 Keep following the markers until you come to Prospect Stile, the highest point of the walk. From here you can clearly see the tump of trees on top of Kelston Round Hill in front of you, and there's a great display which shows you how far away different landmarks are. It's fun trying to spot them on a clear day.

8 From here, the path takes you through a field of infant trees, surrounded by a deer-proof fence, and on up to Kelston Round Hill (about $^1/_2$ mile – 0.8km – from Prospect Stile). You need to divert off the Cotswold Way to reach the hill itself, but it is well worth it because the views are out of this world. On a good day, you should be able to see the Malvern Hills, the Mendips, the Brecon Beacons, both Severn Bridges, Bristol and, of course, Bath. The Beckford monument is clearly visible.

9 By now you deserve a break, so we suggest a rest and relaxation stop, before circling the top of the hill one last time, and heading back the way you came.

10 Alternatively, you could follow the Cotswold Way down into the city of Bath, and catch the bus back to Swineford Picnic Area and the car park. This is an easy, relatively flat and very pretty walk.

Solsbury Hill

A SHORT WALK, A SONG AND DRAMATIC VIEWS OF BATH

Distance: 1³/₄ miles (3 km).

Walking time: 1 hour.

Suitability: Not suitable for buggies, pushchairs or wheelchairs.

Terrain: This is a good one even for quite young children providing they are happy going up hills. There are some good scrambling rocks around the base of the fort. However the track up does get very muddy after prolonged periods of rain so take wellies.

GETTING THERE

From the centre of Bath, take the London Road heading towards the Batheaston bypass. Just before you get there, turn left into Gloucester Road and then take the fifth right into Bailbrook Lane. Drive up the hill for a short distance until you come to Roseland Close (on the right) and you should be able to leave your car on Bailbrook Lane opposite the entrance to the Close.

Dogs: A very good walk for dogs. It also gives them the opportunity to play with some very well bred Bath pedigrees (the last time we climbed Solsbury Hill it was teeming with black Labradors called George and Henry and we also met several springer spaniels!).

Parking: On-street parking on Bailbrook Lane.

Refreshments: None at Solsbury Hill itself. There's a brilliant family restaurant right by the junction of London Road and Gloucester Road and the beautiful city of Bath is just a stone's throw away. Bath, famously, has 365 restaurants so you shouldn't have much trouble finding somewhere to eat before or after.

Toilets: None.

BACKGROUND

PETER GABRIEL WROTE HIS MOST FAMOUS SONG, *Solsbury Hill*, back in 1977. He still lives on this side of Bath and has his own recording studio so you might possibly meet him on this walk. In the interests of information, I looked up the lyrics and the first verse does give an inkling of that top-of-the-world feeling you get on Solsbury Hill. If you'd like to embarrass your offspring while paying tribute to the great British singer/songwriter as you do this walk, it goes like this:

Climbing up on Solsbury Hill/I can see the city lights/Wind was blowing, time stood still/Eagle flew out of the night

In recent times, Solsbury Hill has been in the news for more prosaic reasons. The powers that be decided to build a bypass to carry increasingly heavy traffic away from the village of Batheaston. The lower end of the bypass, to put it crudely, was to cut away the bottom of Solsbury Hill.

There was a huge campaign to prevent work on the bypass going ahead. For months protesters lay down in front of heavy machinery, climbed tower cranes and trees and did everything in their power to save this very special part of the countryside. Sadly their efforts were thwarted in the end and the road now slices through the countryside like a scar.

However, the contractors planted thousands of trees on the banks above the cut-through and these are now beginning to grow.

There are still some remnants of the battle to save Solsbury Hill in the very pretty village of Bailbrook at the foot of the hill. If you follow the lane up into the village either at the beginning or the end of the walk, you come to a most unusual tin church. The church was apparently bought by public subscription in 1892, when the prefabricated tin churches were a popular way of catering for growing populations and congregations. Anyway, on the church roof you can still clearly see the words STOP IT in white paint.

Going much further back in time, Solsbury Hill has been an important site for human beings for thousands of years. There was a walled village on top of the hill during the early iron age and the site was inhabited until about 100 BC. There is still plenty of evidence of the ancient defences put in place by these ancient people.

Aside from all these historical reasons, Solsbury Hill is a magical place. The views are quite out of this world, it's the perfect place to view Bath in all its glory, as well as some of the most beautiful countryside anywhere in England.

1 From Bailbrook Lane, with Roseland Close facing you, turn left and left again up a well-defined track and you actually walk over the top of the bypass. Turn left again, following the footpath signs. The bypass will now be on your left.

2 The path winds up hill. It's quite an easy walk and there are steps in difficult places. Almost immediately you will be struck by the lovely views, it's just a shame about the noise from the traffic below.

3 At the end of the path, you reach a lane. Turn right and follow the lane for just a few yards and then climb over a broken-down stile on the left marked by a footpath sign. Keep to the right side of the field as you walk uphill. At the end of the field climb over the stile and you're now officially on Little Solsbury common.

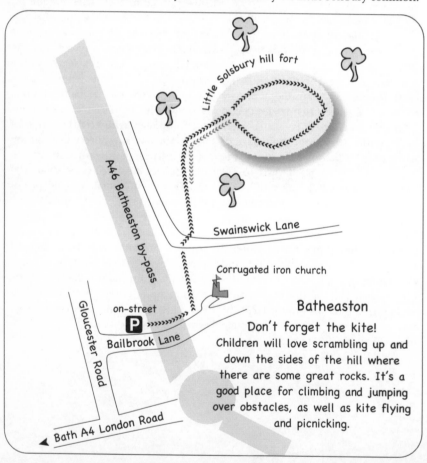

Little Solsbury hill fort

A46 Batheaston by-pass

Swainswick Lane

Corrugated iron church

Gloucester Road

on-street

P

Bailbrook Lane

Bath A4 London Road

Batheaston
Don't forget the kite!
Children will love scrambling up and down the sides of the hill where there are some great rocks. It's a good place for climbing and jumping over obstacles, as well as kite flying and picnicking.

4 Keep going uphill and to the right and you come out into a heath area, which is covered with spongy, grass-covered anthills. Carry on up until you find yourself on the top of Solsbury Hill, just like Peter Gabriel.

It doesn't matter which way you walk round the top, either way you'll find yourself wondering at the views as they unfurl in front of you. From this vantage point, you can look right across Bath and the Avon valley, you can see Bath Racecourse (the highest racecourse in Britain), and Beckford's Tower.

5 It takes quite a while to circuit the hill, and then retrace your footsteps back down to the car park.

6 To divert to Bailbrook, once you're back down on the lane, simply turn left and walk into the village rather than turning right back to the car.

Dundas Aqueduct 10

A WATERSIDE STROLL THROUGH OUR INDUSTRIAL PAST

British Waterways SW Region

Distance: About 2 miles (3.2 km).

Walking time: Allow 2 hours.

Suitability: Not suitable for wheelchair users. There are two points where you have to cross canals by bridge. Carrying a light pushchair or buggy over the bridges wouldn't be difficult. Wheelchair users could not follow this trail, but the canal path leads off in other directions and much of it is accessible.

Terrain: Very easy, level going along a well-maintained path, perfect for even quite small children and people who

GETTING THERE

You need the Bath/Warminster A36 road. Follow the A4 into Bath and then look for signs to Warminster. Or, divert round the back of Bath following signs to Claverton and the American Museum. At the Viaduct Inn traffic lights (about 5 miles – 8km – out of Bath), turn left towards Limpley Stoke on the B3108. After 50 metres, you'll see the Canal Visitor Centre car park on your left.

don't enjoy hills! Obviously you do need to keep an eye on children because of the water. Despite the canal's industrial heritage, this is an exceptionally pretty walk.

Dogs: Well behaved dogs will enjoy this walk. They'll be able to bark at their cousins on the barges.

Parking: Pay-and-display car park at the Canal Visitor Centre.

Refreshments: Café/restaurant.

Toilets: Toilets and baby changing facilities at Brassknocker Basin.

DESIGNED BY JOHN RENNIE, AND NAMED AFTER CHARLES DUNDAS who was the first Chairman of the Kennet and Avon Canal Company, the Dundas Aqueduct carries the Kennet and Avon canal over the River Avon. It doesn't matter how old (or young) you are, you can't fail to be impressed by the sight of long, slow narrowboats passing over this beautiful, classical bridge on a narrow expanse of canal, with the river rushing along a good way below. It's a truly lovely spot.

The aqueduct is actually the solution to a difficult problem. Engineers needed to take the Kennet and Avon canal across the Avon valley between Bath and Bradford-on-Avon, but a valley isn't flat and canals don't work on slopes because all the water would run away. The usual way of making canals operate in areas which aren't flat, is to build locks which cleverly lift (or drop) narrowboats up (or down) the hill. As the Kennet and Avon crosses the Avon valley twice, the engineers came up with the idea of building two aqueducts, to carry the canal over the river instead. The second aqueduct, which isn't so spectacular, is at Avoncliff.

Next to Brassknocker Basin is Dundas Wharf which is where the old Somersetshire Coal Canal meets the Kennet and Avon. Although it's now a private mooring, you can see, and cross, the old canal, which is so narrow you can practically step across it – it's amazing to think that it was of huge industrial significance in the early ⋅1800s. This canal was built because the Somerset miners were worried about competition from the miners of South Wales, who already had a superb canal system for transporting their coal. For many years the Somersetshire Coal Canal supplied most of Bristol and Bath with fuel from the Somerset mines. Unfortunately the project was beset with problems and one section was never finished. Eventually, technology moved on and most coal was transported by rail. Radstock Museum is the place to find out all about the history of coal mining and transport in Somerset.

The wharf is the only undeveloped wharf remaining on the Kennet and Avon and is of great social and historical importance.

The canal company made its money from charging all the craft which used the canal, hence the old toll office. At the wharf, gauging blocks were craned onto the boats, and the amount of toll to be paid was calculated according to the amount of water displaced. Enthusiasts are currently trying to restore this valuable part of our industrial heritage.

If you don't feel like walking, you could always explore the Kennet and Avon canal by narrowboat instead. The narrowboat *Jubilee* operates out of Brassknocker Basin with public trips every Good Friday, Sundays and Bank Holidays from Easter to the end of October, plus Tuesday and Thursday trips from June until September.

Departures are 12 noon to Claverton, returning at 2pm, and 2.30pm to Avoncliff, returning at 5.45pm. There are additional afternoon summer trips. For more information and prices visit www.bath-narrowboat-trips.co.uk or tel. 01749 850169. Just as well to check in case times, etc change.

You could walk anywhere you wished along the side of the canal, but the old pumping station at Claverton is of great interest in its own right and it's a pleasant 40-minute walk from Brassknocker Basin.

1 From the Canal Visitor Centre and Brassknocker Basin, with the canal on your left, follow the path until you reach the aqueduct. It's worth walking over the aqueduct and, if you're lucky, watching a narrowboat glide over the bridge.

2 Then retrace your footsteps a little and follow the signs to Claverton. You will cross a bridge over the narrow coal canal and then, a little further up, cross the canal again, so that you're walking along the towpath with the canal to your left.

There is so much to see that nobody will be bored. The boats themselves are fascinating. Many of them are in the process of being restored, and the traditional paintwork and copper accessories are on display. Others have gardens on the top, or sleeping dogs, or smoking chimneys, or washing lines. Some are moored at the

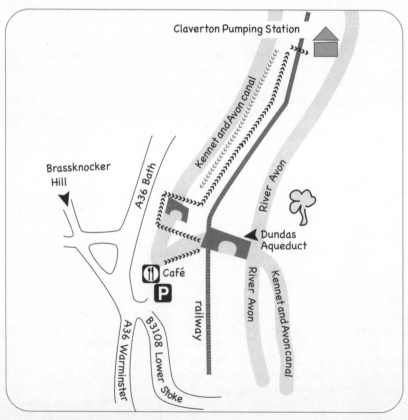

side of the canal, others will drift past you. It's impossible not to envy the people on board, most of whom look very relaxed and friendly.

3 To your right is the river Avon, lovely at any time of year. How much of it you can see will depend on the time of year you walk and the amount of tree cover – but don't worry because you'll get some very good views at the Pumping Station! There's also a railway line to your right.

4 Follow the canal until you reach Claverton Pumping Station. You have to divert off the canal towpath at this point and follow the signs leading down the road. The Pumping Station fulfils an extremely important function, and has done so for nearly 200 years. At Bath, the canal drops down to the river Avon by means of a flight of six locks (there used to be seven). Every time a boat goes through these locks, thousands of gallons of water drains from the canal into the river.

To replace this lost water, John Rennie sited a pumping station at Claverton, one powerful enough to lift 100,000 gallons of water an hour from the river into the canal, more than 12m above. It's brilliantly effective, because the pump is operated by a giant waterwheel which is powered by the river. So water is pumped into the canal from the river at Claverton, and the same water goes back into the river at Bath.

If you want to go inside the Pump House, it's open to the public every Sunday, Wednesday and Bank Holiday from Easter to Autumn. Visit www.claverton.org or telephone 01225 483001 for exact times, dates and admission prices. At the time of writing, accompanied children under 16 can visit the station for free. There are also a number of days every year when the pump is operational.

5 After you've admired the Pump House, it's a question of going back the way you came. You can't get back to Brassknocker Basin (or to anywhere for that matter) by walking along the side of the river, so go back up to the canal and enjoy the views from the opposite direction. When you reach the Visitor Centre, we can personally recommend the tea and cakes.

www.claverton.org tel: 01225 483001   www.bath-narrowboat-trips.co.uk

Wellow

11

A LONG AND LOVELY WALK TO A FIVE THOUSAND-YEAR-OLD BURIAL CHAMBER

Distance: About 8 miles (12 km).

Walking time: Allow around 4 hours.

Suitability: Not suitable for buggies, push-chairs or wheelchairs.

Terrain: This walk is most suitable for older children. Although none of it is particularly arduous, it would be too long for small children. Some parts of the walk are extremely muddy in winter, particularly the first stretch up the farm track.

GETTING THERE

Take the A367 south from Bath heading out towards Radstock. Turn eastwards off the Peasedown St John bypass and follow the signs to Wellow.

Dogs: A good, long walk for dogs but be aware of livestock in some of the fields.

Parking: On-street parking or there is a free car park in the village.

Refreshments: The walk starts and ends at the very pleasant Fox and Badger pub at Wellow which welcomes families with and without dogs. The pub has its own website ww.foxandbadger.co.uk so you can check opening times. Wellow is a small village and facilities are limited, but you are only a short drive from a host of other towns and villages and just six miles (9.5km) from Bath. As this is a long trek, we would recommend taking some food and drink with you, as there's nowhere to buy refreshments en route.

Toilets: No public toilets.

As a family, this is one of our favourite walks because it has everything from old railway lines to a ford, a fantastically intact 5,000-year-old burial chamber, a lovely river, Second World War defences, amazing views and everything else you'd want from a good, long, weekend country trail.

We were shown this walk by a friend who used to live in Bath, and quite a few things have changed since the first time we did it. Most noticeably, there's a huge housing estate being built where once there were just fields.

If you don't feel like doing the whole walk, we'd still highly recommend going as far as the burial barrow. The remains of this Neolithic shrine are so well preserved that they look as if they could have been built yesterday. In fact, the mound was built 5,000 years ago and probably served the local farming community. At the end of the mound is a central gallery with three pairs of side chambers which is where the bodies were buried. According to the notice board beside the mound, the barrow would probably have been used for hundreds of years.

Not being archaeologists, we couldn't work out how this was possible, as there is not much room inside the chamber, and you would have thought it would have filled up pretty quickly. If you're more than about one metre tall, you'll have to crawl inside but it is worth a look and is of great interest to adults and children alike – if a little scary.

Of equal interest are the tank traps in the stream further along the walk. It seems odd that people in the middle of Somerset were so worried about being invaded that they built concrete defences to stop tanks storming into their villages, but there was, at the time, a genuine fear that Hitler would invade via the south-west coast. The defences were put in the stream because people feared tanks would enter the village that way if the locals blew up the bridge to stop them using the road.

Finally, the walk is dotted with bridges and arches that were built during the golden age of the railways and which, sadly, are no longer in use. And that's a real shame because the only way to reach Wellow now is by road.

1 Start from the Fox and Badger pub which, according to legend, got its name because the locals couldn't agree whether to call it The Fox, or The Badger, and so reached a compromise. It's the only pub in the country with this name. You'll see the Railway Lane sign on the front of the pub.

2 With the pub on your right, follow the road. Take the first turning right into Mill Hill and walk downhill to the ford. The ford can be quite deep if there's been a lot of rain, and you won't want to get your feet wet this early on in the walk so cross over the bridge to the right instead. Keep to the right and, a couple of hundred metres later, the road bends sharply to the left. You want to bear right, don't take the left fork. In front of you, you'll see a farm track. Follow this track uphill until you reach the gate at the top.

3 Keep walking straight on, along the track and through the next field. With the field edge to your left, walk along the field until you can see the burial mound in a fenced enclosure to your right. Walk across the field and you'll see the stile going into the enclosure.

4 Once you've spent enough time at the barrow, leave the enclosure via the stile to the left, and walk across the next field bearing left towards the stile. From

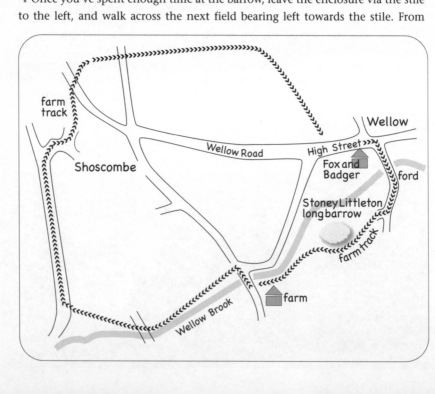

here, walk downhill to the gate leading into the farmyard. Follow the track past the farm and you soon reach a lane. Turn right, cross the bridge over the river and walk up the road.

5 Soon you reach a stile on you left. Go over the stile and into the field. Now you have a lovely walk through the river valley, following the line of Wellow Brook keeping the river on your left. Keep going over another stile, along a little lane and into a minor road. Turn left and pass over the river bridge. This is where you'll see the pyramid-shaped anti-tank defences.

6 Follow the road up the hill. You soon reach two houses on either side of the road and here you need to follow the signed footpath to the right of the house on your right. You feel like you're walking through the garden of the house (in fact you are) but it is your right of way. Go over the stile into the field beyond and cross it. There's a stile into the second field, and a third. At this point, walk directly towards a house with the hedge on your left.

7 Climb over the metal gate into a lane. In front of you is Foxcote Church of St James the Less. Turn right and follow the lane downhill. At the bottom, there's a further reminder of the railway line, a row of arches where the railway bridge used to stand. Follow the road uphill and, at the next junction, turn right, following the signs for Shoscombe. Soon you'll reach a sharp, right-hand bend. Don't go round the bend, instead go up the track in front of you.

8 At the metal gate, there are two tracks, take the right-hand one (not into the yard by the old barn though). It takes you along to another road. Cross the road and go over the stile into the field where there is massive development taking place. Follow the designated footpath through the site until you meet another road. Cross this road and go through the furthest right-hand gate. After a while the bridleway goes into an enclosed track and you simply follow this until you cross a large track marked by a big barn. This is a really nice part of the walk, with the most gorgeous views over the valleys.

9 Go right here, and after about 300 metres climb over the wooden stile into the large field on your right. There's a wood in the dip beyond. Head diagonally across this field keeping to the left of the wood. You'll find a wooden stile just above the far right-hand corner of the field. Walk across to the hedge ahead and go through the gate into the next field. Walk downhill, keeping the hedge on your left, and then head down towards the barn. There's a metal gate to the left of the barn and you're back out onto the road that leads into Wellow.

Stanton Drew

12

A MYSTICAL STONE CIRCLE

Distance: About 1$^1/_2$ miles (2km).

Walking time: Less than an hour.

Suitability: Although it would be impossible to manage buggies, pushchairs and wheelchairs on the land where the Stanton Drew stones stand, they could be parked at the entrance to the field.

Terrain: A very easy walk, suitable for all. There is a small section of walking on unpaved roads.

Dogs: No dogs allowed.

Parking: There's a car park at the entrance to the main stone circle site but it is in the middle of a small housing estate and visitors are asked to leave cars there for the minimum time. We recommend leaving your car in the second, small car park on the left-hand side of the road just past the Druid's Arms pub.

Refreshments: Druid's Arms is a nice pub with a garden, and is one of the few pubs in the world which can boast three massive great standing stones in its garden (although one of them is actually lying down!) There are some lovely pubs in nearby Chew Magna and just about any of the villages in the Chew Valley. If you want to combine the walk with a visit to Chew Valley Lake, then visit the restaurant at the visitor centre where there are toilets, picnic benches, and lovely views across the water.

Toilets: No public toilets.

GETTING THERE

Depending on which side of Bristol you live, either take the A37 or the A38. Either way, you need to get on to the B3130 (road to Chew Magna). When you reach the little toll house take the road past it towards Stanton Drew. Follow the lane into the village, and follow the heritage signs to The Cove. This brings you past the Druid's Arms pub directly to the small car park.

BACKGROUND

Everybody knows what the standing stones at Stonehenge look like and most people have at least heard of the Avebury stone circles, even if they've never been there.

But right on our doorstep is an equally impressive megalithic site, consisting of one of the most important stone circles in the world: Stanton Drew.

Quite why these fantastic circles remain so unknown is a mystery in itself. They are a little bit off the beaten track (although only $5^1/_2$ miles (9km) from the centre of Bristol so not exactly in the middle of nowhere), and although they're in the care of English Heritage, they are sited on private land which might explain why they are such a well kept secret.

Little is known about the stone circles at Stanton Drew although they have been described as the 'most important prehistoric monument in Somerset' and the larger of the two main circles, the Great Circle, is the second largest in Britain after Avebury.

There are three stone circles. The Great Circle is the first one you see, and the stones are so spread out that it's a little difficult, from the ground, to recognise the circle. Just behind this one is the north-east circle with some spectacular stones, and the south-west circle lies a little way beyond.

As well as the circles, there are some freestanding sarsens which may have been part of two avenues.

There is a separate group of three large megaliths in the garden of the Druid's Arms pub which are known as the Cove and also as the 'bride, bridegroom and priest'.

To the north, across the river Chew, is a single stone called Hautville's Quoit which is believed to be all that remains of a burial chamber or other large structure. (In the interests of research, *Children's Bristol* went to explore Hautville's Quoit and all you can see is a lumpy patch of rock in the ground so don't make a special journey!)

Stone circles are known to date back to the late Neolithic and early Bronze Age (around 3,000 to 2,000 BC). The circles are thought to have played an important part in the lives of the people of that era, either for social or religious functions, or both.

English Heritage recently conducted a geophysical survey of the Stanton Drew site. If you watch Time Team, you'll know that this is a way of measuring magnetic anomalies within the soil to plot the presence of buried features, including pits and ditches. The results were astonishing and show that the stones that remain at Stanton Drew are just a small part of a much more elaborate and important site. Beneath the field where the Great Circle stands lie buried pits, arranged in nine concentric rings with the stone circle at the centre. It was also revealed that the circle itself is contained within a very deep ditch.

Science aside, there are some interesting legends about Stanton Drew. One claims the stones are actually the remains of revellers and musicians who were dancing in circles at the wedding of the bride and groom when the Devil cast a spell upon them, turning them to stone. That's why we have the bride, groom and priest in the pub garden.

1 Steps from the car park lead to the back entrance of the Druid's Arms pub garden. Right in front of you, you'll see three huge sarsens, the bride, the groom and the priest. One of these is lying on the floor and is creepily human in shape, although as big as a giant. Once you've admired these stones, turn round back down the steps and turn right into the road.

2 Walk past the pub, and take the first turning on your right and then follow the lane round into a small housing estate to Court Farm. You will feel as if you are walking through private property, but this is the only way to get to the Great Circle.

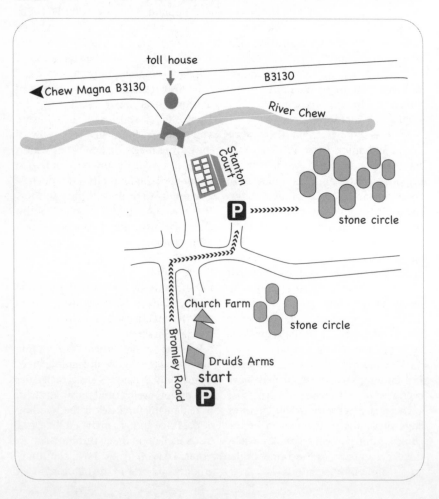

3 At the car park, there's a gate through into a yard. There's an honesty box at the gate in the car park, and admission costs £1. The circles are open during daylight hours all year round. Once through the gate, walk through the farmyard and go through the kissing gate to enter the site itself. Don't be put off by the livestock. They're used to being stared at.

4 It is well worth taking the time to walk all the way round the site, as some of the larger stones are the furthest away and the remains of the north-east circle are very impressive indeed.

The site is something of a magnet to New Age travellers and old hippies, and you'll understand why when you go there and touch the stones and feel the history of the place. As for children, see if they can count the stones, or work out how their ancestors managed to stand them up without any machinery.

If you've timed it right, we suggest you retrace your steps and enjoy some well-earned refreshments in the Druid's Arms garden.

Can you count the stones? Like the trees in Winnie the Pooh's hundred-acre wood, legend says that every time you count the stones, you end up with a different number.

Ebbor Gorge

13

A BEAUTIFUL LIMESTONE GORGE

Distance: About $2^1/_2$ miles (4 km).

Walking time: $1^1/_2$–2 hours.

Suitability: Not suitable for buggies, pushchairs or wheelchairs.

Terrain: There are several walks at Ebbor Gorge. The one described in detail here is best suited for the over-sevens as there's a section which involves scrambling up rocks which active children aged seven to 14+ will enjoy. It's not suitable for really small children or for anyone carrying a baby. With all respect to grannies and grampies, stretches can be hard-going – but we do offer an easier detour.

You will need good boots with grip to complete this walk safely. There is an easier path which avoids the tricky section, and we've included directions for that too. There's a third, alternative walk which is specifically for people with buggies and/or wheelchairs. A map of this walk is on display in the grassy area at the side of the car park.

Dogs: Dogs are welcome but they must be kept on a lead for their own safety and for the protection of wildlife.

Parking: There's a free National Trust car park at the start of the walk

Refreshments: There's a café/restaurant at Wookey Hole caves, and the nearby Wookey Hole Inn does good food. There are two pubs in nearby Priddy. The city of Wells is only a couple of miles away, and is packed with cafés, bars and restaurants.

Toilets: No public toilets at Ebbor Gorge itself.

There are several separate grassy areas which are perfect for picnics either at the beginning or the end of the walk.

GETTING THERE

From Bristol, take the A39 Wells Road and follow it until you're almost in Wells. Turn right at the roundabout and then take the road to Cheddar. At the traffic lights, there's a right turn signposted Wookey Hole. Follow the lane through the village and past the entrance to the caves and continue on up a fairly steep hill with lovely views on either side. After about half a mile (0.8km), towards the top of the hill, on the right-hand side is a well marked car park.

The views are out of this world. Wookey Hole caves are just down the road so a visit to the caves followed by a picnic and a walk round Ebbor Gorge would make a perfect family day out.

Warning! This is a gorge and there are some steep cliffs. There are also some dangerous scree slopes at the lowest point of the gorge and it's not safe for children to play in the caves.

THE FIRST TIME WE VISITED EBBOR GORGE NATIONAL TRUST NATURE RESERVE we were quite blown away by the sheer beauty of the place. It's probably the least known gorge in the area, yet it's in an area of outstanding beauty at any time of year, and one of a number of really lovely family walking places between Wells and Cheddar.

Ebbor Gorge was created by the same geological processes that gave us the caves at Cheddar and Wookey and the other dramatic gorges carved into the limestone hills of that part of Somerset. These processes began nearly 300 million years ago, and their continuing effects can be seen today.

Slightly acid rainwater seeps into cracks in the limestone and gradually dissolves and wears away at the rock to form caves or increasingly deep valleys. When the hollowing of the rocks takes place underground, the water will eventually emerge as a spring or from the mouth of a cave. Sometimes huge caverns are created, and when the roofs collapse, we are left with interesting and unusual outdoor rock formations.

Walking through Ebbor Gorge, it's easy to imagine yourself back in prehistory seeing the world through the eyes of the earliest human beings. The plants and scenery and the stream that runs underfoot in Hope Wood Valley reminded my son of the film *Jurassic Park*.

There are several caves and rock shelters in the gorge where the remains of reindeer, bears, wolves and lemmings have been discovered. Later on, Neolithic people lived in the caves and

you can still see their tools and ornaments in the museums at Wookey Hole and at Wells.

The gorge is also a haven for birds, insects, flowers and all manner of wildlife. The woods are mainly ash and oak, but also whitebeam, wych elm and others. If you hear a drumming noise, yes that's almost certainly one of the resident woodpeckers. In spring, look out for bluebells, wood anemones and violets.

1 Climb over the stone stile at the back of the car park and follow the path down between the trees climbing down the shallow, man-made steps.

2 At the path T-junction, follow the red arrow along the left-hand path signposted 'The Gorge'. Cross the stream via the wooden bridge and at the next T-junction turn left again, following the red arrow. Or, take the easier route described below.*

3 This path takes you into the gorge itself. You'll find yourself walking between sheer limestone cliffs, covered with trees. The ground underfoot is likely to be very wet, as a spring emerges halfway up the climb ahead so you will be walking through water for some of the way.

4 The path becomes more arduous as it climbs up the far side of the gorge, it's very rocky and steep and narrow. As you walk/scramble up, you'll probably want to stop and look back down the gorge – and, if you're an older member of the outing, take a well-earned breather! There are some exciting caves to the side and children enjoy discovering the source of the spring which magically appears from beneath a natural step in the path. At the top, there are spectacular views back over the gorge. In front of you, you'll see a T-junction marked with a fallen tree.

*Ignore the red arrow and take the right-hand path. Simply follow the path up round the gorge. There are some steps but these are far less arduous. Eventually, you'll come to the junction with the path up from the gorge. To your right is a fallen tree.

5 With your back to the gorge, ignore the red sign to the car park. Instead, take the narrow, left-hand path uphill between the trees. At the top, there's a stile to climb over. You will see immediately to your right another stile and direction arrow – ignore this! Instead, turn left, following the line of the woods and keeping them on your left. From now on, there are lovely and spectacular views.

6 At the field boundary, there's another stile marked with a yellow arrow. Cross this field and follow the path across a tumbledown drystone wall and head towards the stile off to your left, again marked with a yellow arrow.

You should now be in a very pretty, historic landscape with views to your left stretching into the far distance. You should be able to see Glastonbury Tor. There are flowers and butterflies here in spring and summer, berries and fungi in autumn, and uninterrupted views in winter when the leaves have fallen.

7 The path leads through a gap in the hedge and after a few metres it turns left down the hill. There is an arrow but it's close to the ground and sometimes hard to spot and the path is not well trodden – head for the wooden post at the bottom of the hill.

8 You're now back in the woods. Turn right over the stile and follow the path which loops around and starts to climb again. From this point, ignore the yellow arrows and just follow the path, which will take you back to the car park. There is a viewing point across the gorge at the top of the hill which is a good place to stop for a breather.

AN EXCURSION TO PRIDDY

When your walk is over and you are leaving the car park, you might care to turn right and take the very pleasant road to the strange village of Priddy, and from there either meander back to Bristol or rejoin the Wells road off to the right. Priddy Fair, which used to be held in Wells, before the ravages of the Black Death saw it shifted to the heights of Priddy, is held annually on the Wednesday nearest to August 21. It's worth a stroll round, and there are two good pubs, including The Queen Victoria, with a most elegant hanging sign.

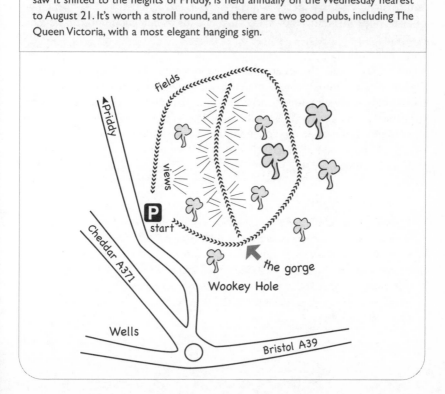

Charterhouse 14

A BEAUTIFUL AND STRANGE LANDSCAPE

Distance: About $1^1/_2$ miles (3km).

Walking time: About $1^1/_2$ hours.

Suitability: There are lots of walks around Charterhouse and the neighbouring Velvet Bottom. This one is not suitable for buggies, pushchairs or wheelchairs but there is a specially surfaced trail around the Blackmoor reserve which is. For a map of the trail contact the Mendip Hills AONB Service at the Charterhouse Centre, tel: 01761 462338 or visit: www.mendiphillsaonb.org.uk

Parking: On-road parking.

Refreshments and toilets: There are toilets at the Charterhouse Centre. Cheddar Gorge is just a few miles away, with plenty of shops, cafés, restaurants, family-friendly pubs, a great ice-cream parlour, public toilets and its own range of attractions including the caves. There are also some good pubs in Blagdon and Shipham.

Dogs: Will love it.

Warning! This walk crosses and borders land which has been extensively used for lead working since before Roman times. Exposed mine shafts are capped and fenced off but are sometimes opened by potholers and there may still be some unmarked shafts. The ponds are extremely deep and don't let children play with the soil as it is poisonous. If you are unlucky enough to be bitten by an adder, seek medical help immediately. (Don't let all this put you off – it's a beautiful walk and well worth doing!)

> **GETTING THERE**
>
> Charterhouse lies about midway between Blagdon and Cheddar. Follow the signed lanes from the B3134 from Burrington Combe or the B3371 from West Harptree.

Mendip Walks

If you want to do more walks in the Mendips, but don't know where to start, we recommend contacting Richard MacDonnell of Mendip Guided Walks. Richard leads a range of walks over all parts of the Mendips and is a mine of historical and anecdotal information. Walks can be tailored to suit different ages and abilities. There is a small charge per person.

For more information, contact Mendip Guided Walks on: 01934 852263 or email: richard.macd@ukgateway.net.

THIS PART OF THE COUNTRYSIDE IS AN OFFICIAL AREA OF OUTSTANDING NATURAL BEAUTY and probably unique in its topography and industrial history. It's a wildlife haven and place of perfect peace now, but from prehistoric times right up to the Victorian era, it teemed with miners, extracting lead from the land. With all the refining and smelting and associated industrial activities, it must have been noisy, busy and smoky.

You can still see the remains of the old Roman hill fort and the settlement where the workforce lived.

Much of the land is covered with hillocks and shafts. In Somerset speak, this is known as 'gruffy ground' and it's what's left of the old mining activities. The ground still contains high levels of lead, zinc and cadmium, giving the grass a peculiar yellow tinge. It's not a good idea to ingest any of these substances, so we recommend picnicking in the car.

The exposed landscape today was left behind by the early Victorians who reworked the area for lead that had been left first-time round. They refined and re-smelted the existing debris and sank more shafts. Look out for the circular 'buddles' where ore was refined, slag heaps and settling ponds. Because of its history, the whole area has been designated as an Ancient Monument of national importance.

Because much of the land is toxic, there are relatively few plants and animals tough enough to live on the Reserve, but those that do are thriving. Rare plants like Alpine Pennycress have developed enough tolerance to colonise the old slag heaps and beautiful Marsh Marigolds thrive on the edges of the ponds as do the water-loving alder trees.

The ponds are also home to hundreds of frogs, many of which end up as dinner for the grass snakes which hunt in the open water. There are also a good number of adders living in the nooks and crannies of the hillocks and shafts and an awful lot of rabbits.

The reserve is owned by Somerset County Council and is about 240 metres above sea level which makes it one of the highest walks in this book. On a good day, the views can be spectacular.

1 There is plenty of room for parked cars at the side of the lane where the walk starts. You can also leave cars in the car park behind the Charterhouse Centre. Turn into the lane that runs along the side of the building past the wind pump, and continue to the parking area marked as P2 on the map.

2 If you have parked on the lane (P1) go through the gate marked by a 'public footpath' sign and follow the path beside the wire fence. Beyond the fence, you can see right down into the old mine workings, and the layers that have been cut through the land by the ancient miners. At the end of the path, you'll come to another gate leading into the alternative parking area.

3 The raised area opposite the gate is part of the old Roman settlement. Although there are some trees growing out of the ground, you can still make out the shape of the earthworks, and realise what good views there must have been from the top. Below are the ditches where the Romans used to do their smelting.

4 Now walk past the information board and over the high stile – the path is marked 'public footpath'. Follow the grass path as it curls uphill. To your right, is the entrance to a mine which is still used by potholers seeking underground adventure. It's surrounded by a high mesh fence to stop people and animals falling in.

For most of the year, there is a fantastic array of rare wildflowers at each side of the path, and hundreds of rabbits live here. If you go in the early evening you'll be dazzled by all the flashes of white tail as they dash out of your way.

5 At the top of the hill, the path meets a lovely old drystone wall. Keeping the wall to your left, follow it for a couple of hundred yards until you reach another stile. Climb over this and you'll find yourself in a landscape as strange and beautiful as anything you saw in *Lord of the Rings* trilogy.

6 Walk around the area as you wish, there's no obvious designated footpath at the top of the field. To return to your car, just keep heading in a vaguely downhill and right direction and you'll eventually either join the path at the far end of the field, or meet the wall which protects the old mine workings from this side. Follow either boundary and you'll come to a gate out on to the lane.

People who left their cars behind the Charterhouse Centre will have to double back through the far gate.

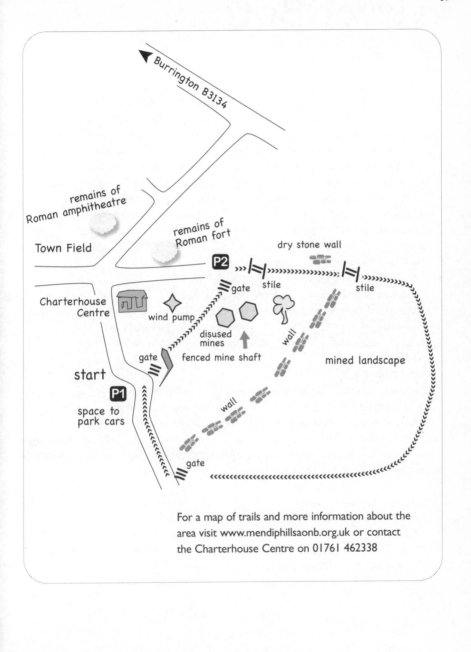

Burrington B3134

remains of
Roman amphitheatre

Town Field

remains of
Roman fort

dry stone wall

P2

gate   stile   stile

Charterhouse
Centre

wind pump

disused
mines

fenced mine shaft

wall

mined landscape

start

gate

P1

space to
park cars

wall

wall

gate

For a map of trails and more information about the
area visit www.mendiphillsaonb.org.uk or contact
the Charterhouse Centre on 01761 462338

Velvet Bottom 15

A WALK THROUGH ROMAN BRITAIN

THIS WALK STARTS AND ENDS AT THE SAME PLACE as the Charterhouse Walk, but is worth doing in its own right. The facilities, directions and warning about the dangers of potholes and lead poisoning still apply. If you want to, you can start from the other end of the walk, at Black Rock. There's room to park cars off the B3135 road (the road which runs through Cheddar Gorge).

Distance: 2 miles (3km).

Walking time: 1–1$\frac{1}{2}$ hours, depending on how far you want to walk.

Suitability: Not suitable for buggies, pushchairs or wheelchairs but there is a specially surfaced trail around the Blackmoor reserve which is. For a map of the trail contact the Mendip Hills AONB Service at the Charterhouse Centre, tel: 01761 462338 or visit: www.mendiphillsaonb.org.uk

Terrain: This is not a difficult walk, although it would be too challenging for very small children.

Dogs: Will love it.

Warning! This walk crosses and borders land which has been extensively used for lead working since before Roman times. Exposed mine shafts are capped and fenced off but are sometimes opened by potholers and there may still be some unmarked shafts. The ponds are extremely deep and don't let children play with the soil as it is poisonous. If you are unlucky enough to be bitten by an adder, seek medical help immediately. (Don't let all this put you off – it's a beautiful walk and well worth doing!)

Parking: On-road parking.

Refreshments: Cheddar Gorge is just a few miles away, with plenty of shops, cafés, restaurants, family-friendly pubs, a great ice-cream parlour, public toilets and its own range of attractions including the caves. There are also some good pubs in Blagdon and Shipham.

Toilets: At the Charterhouse Centre.

> **GETTING THERE**
> Charterhouse lies about midway between Blagdon and Cheddar. Follow the signed lanes from the B3134 from Burrington Combe or the B3371 from West Harptree. Alternatively take the B3135 through Cheddar.

> **Help!** We don't know how Velvet Bottom got its name (but if anybody knows, please email us via our website: www.childrensbristol.co.uk).

THIS WALK STARTS AT THE CAR PARK AT CHARTERHOUSE and takes you on a journey through the history both of the Mendips and of Rome.

While the Charterhouse walk takes you though much of the land that was mined for lead first by the Romans, and then by the Victorians, this one literally follows the bed of the man-made river which was used to wash and separate the lead from its ore. For much of the walk, you are quite clearly walking along a river bed, and one that was so polluted by heavy metal, that even today only grass will grow in it, so it has the appearance of being mowed and manicured.

Few people are aware that there is a genuine Roman amphitheatre up on the Mendips, the remains of which are still clearly visible if you know where to look.

If you walk back towards the Charterhouse centre from the car park, ahead of you, across the lane, you'll see a field and there, clearly defined is the amphitheatre. The huge Roman workforce brought in to mine the Mendips would, of course, have needed somewhere to relax and chill out, and they would have expected entertainment to be laid on. Hence the amphitheatre. Quite a thought, people sitting there all those centuries ago, enjoying their very own Frankie Howards.

It must have been extremely chilly out there for the greater part of the year (the amphitheatre may still be impressive, but it's stuck on the side of a wind-blown hill a long way from the sunny Mediterranean), and it's likely that in the winter months, the amphi-theatre would have been used for meetings as well as to put on plays.

The field in which the amphitheatre stands is called 'Town Field' in honour of the fact that it was, hundreds of years ago, a bustling Roman town and home to hundreds of people.

The Romans were not mining the lead for the benefit of the natives of the land they had invaded. It was exported to Rome where a massive programme of building work was going on. The material was needed for piping and other purposes. Analysis of the lead in existing Roman buildings proves that it came from the Charterhouse areas and has been recycled in Rome ever since.

On the other side of the lane, you can make out the shape of the Roman fort. You'll also notice that the lanes around the area are perfectly straight. They were, of course, Roman-built roads.

A little way further along the lane is what looks like a church hall, but is in fact St Hugh's chapel. Long after the Romans left, the Victorians moved back into the site to rework the material the Romans had left behind. Originally simply a miners' hall, the building was converted into a chapel by a kindly Christian benefactor in the early 1900s.

It's not much to look at from the outside, but it's still a working chapel and the interior is outstanding. It contains what some claim is the finest example of twentieth-century wood carving in Britain – if you peep through the windows you might be able to see it.

Outside the chapel is a cross with an image of St Hugh of Avalon carved at the top, together with his pet swan. How a French-born saint ended up being commemorated in a wild corner of Somerset is quite a long story which begins with Henry II.

He wanted to found a Carthusian foundation at Witham in Somerset but things kept going wrong. Hearing about Hugh, who, at the time, was procurator (one of the top monks) of the Grande-Chartreuse in France – a monastery famous for the extreme piety of its monks – King Henry managed to persuade him to come to England to help him out, probably in 1175.

Hugh's first sensible move was to insist that the king pay compensation to the villagers who had been turned out of their houses to make way for the monastery. He went on to grow it into a thriving foundation and in 1186, Henry appointed him bishop of Lincoln.

Hugh's pet swan was a legend in its own lifetime. For 14 years, the swan would accurately predict Hugh's arrival by becoming increasingly animated. It followed him everywhere when he was around, and then returned to the wild when he departed.

Charterhouse actually got its name from 'Chartreuse' because of the St Hugh connection.

Those clever Romans needed a way to carry the heavy lead down from the mines on the higher ground at Charterhouse and the most logical solution was to build a canal. All those years ago, the Mendips would have been even wetter than they are today, and it wouldn't have been difficult to divert little streams into the path of the canal. The whole area would be flooded, and then drained, leaving the heavy lead ore to be collected at the bottom of a series of 'buddle pits' – circular pits sunk into the channel constructed to hold the water.

It's exactly like walking along an old river bed. From time to time you pass piles of old smelting waste, black glass that was the by-product of the process.

1 From the car park marked on the map, turn back down the lane, past the windmill, and head towards the Charterhouse Centre. As you walk down the lane, look to your right and over the opposite lane, you can see Town Field and the Roman amphitheatre.

2 At the junction, turn left and walk along to St Hugh's chapel. The start of the walk is a short way beyond this on the right-hand side of the road. The walk is well signed. If you follow the valley through the ravine, there is ample evidence of all the mining and lead production activity that used to go on there.
Apart from this, the area is a haven for wild birds, including buzzards, and rabbits who aren't particularly afraid of people.

3 The canal channel leads you uninterrupted down to a stile and from here you can continue to follow it to Black Rock, a dramatic slice of rock. Carry on past Black Rock and eventually you reach the road which winds down the Cheddar Gorge.

4 Alternatively, you can divert at the stile either to the right, up to the Long Wood Reserve, or to the left, following a path which climbs up the side of the valley and eventually brings you back out to the lane.

5 You now have another choice. You can either cross the lane and walk back to the car park via the old mine-worked land described in the Charterhouse walk, or follow the (exceedingly quiet) lane back down to the Charterhouse Centre.

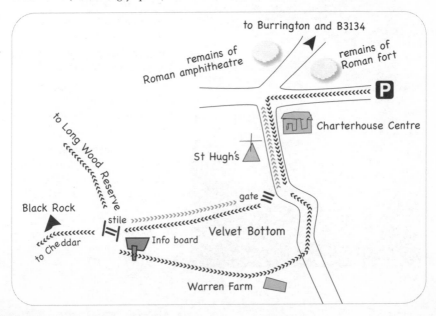

to Burrington and B3134

remains of Roman amphitheatre

remains of Roman fort

P

Charterhouse Centre

to Long Wood Reserve

St Hugh's

Black Rock

to Cheddar

stile

gate

Info board

Velvet Bottom

Warren Farm

Goblin Combe

16

A STRENUOUS WALK IN ONE OF ENGLAND'S LOVELIEST LANDSCAPES

Distance: About $2^1/_2$ miles (4km).

Walking time: 2 hours.

Suitability: Not suitable for wheelchairs or pushchairs.

Terrain: This is probably the most challenging walk in this book with a climb up a very steep, narrow, stepped path. It is not suitable for very small children although more adventurous youngsters will relish the climb. Also, it doesn't matter what time of year you go, or how many days since it last rained, but the path at the bottom of the gorge is always muddy and slippery in patches – wear decent footwear.

Facilities: The Lord Nelson pub, two or three stones' throw from the start of the walk, is very family-friendly with a large garden, well-equipped outdoor play area and a big restaurant serving the good-value 'chips and burgers'-style Hungry Horse menu. There are several other good pubs nearby: head to Congresbury or Backwell for a more eclectic selection.

Toilets: There are no public toilets.

Dogs: A good walk for dogs but keep them away from cliff edges.

Warning! This walk peaks in what are probably the best views in North Somerset but you will be standing at the top of a gorge – please take care near cliff edges.

GETTING THERE

Take the A370 (Long Ashton bypass) out of Bristol and carry on through Farleigh and Backwell into Cleeve. Immediately past the Japanese car import centre and immediately before the Lord Nelson pub, turn left into Cleeve Hill Road, a small lane. After a couple of hundred metres, you'll see a small car park on your left. Park here.

BACKGROUND

THE **BBC** WEBSITE has an area where people can nominate their favourite part of England. It's not surprising that Goblin Combe features fairly prominently on this talk board. It seems that to find and experience this magical place is to love it – but it does take some effort to find it!

The Combe is actually yet another limestone gorge, and it's situated in the wooded area directly beneath a flight path to Bristol International Airport. Depending on your point of view, this can be regarded as a very good, or a very bad thing. During your walk, the peace, quiet, birdsong and fluttering of butterflies will, fairly regularly, be interrupted by the boom of jet engines as aeroplanes take off. It is actually quite exciting seeing planes from directly underneath and my boys really enjoyed counting the minutes in between jets.

Part of the Forest of Avon, the area is also home to the Goblin Combe Environment Centre, an excellent facility for both locals and visiting groups, which organises nature walks, and other conservation and environmental-focussed events. Avon Wildlife Trust also has a reserve there.

The area is of great historic importance, about half of it designated a Site of Special Scientific Interest. The trees are predominantly yew, some of them many hundreds of years old, and you'll see plenty of carboniferous lime–stone, the unique Goblin Combe Oolite (limestone made of millions of tiny, egg-like particles) and natural scree. The stone was quarried hundreds of years ago to build roads.

The woodland is ancient and the whole environment is rare, and special. The site is nationally important for butterflies and the scarce species of limestone fern which thrives there.

There's also an unexcavated hillfort hidden by trees and undergrowth in the woods. It dates back to the late Bronze Age (around the eighth century BC) but I'm afraid you can't see it.

So why Goblin Combe? There are a handful of legends. For hundreds of years, people have believed that goblins lived in the gorge. Although they are supposed to be mischievous and sometimes downright nasty creatures, on more than one occasion a goblin is said to have materialised out of the undergrowth to help children who were lost in the Combe. You can still see the stones where they used to sit and eat their dinner round a slab table at the top of the series of steps leading up the right side of the Combe.

Goblin Combe may be in North Somerset, but it does have an atmosphere of 'deepest, darkest' about it and it's very easy to be spooked by rustling and scurrying in the undergrowth, especially at dusk.

Furthermore, according to the *Fortean Times* (the magazine of weird and wonderful goings-on) a first-class goblin specimen was spotted in the Combe as recently as 2002.

1 From the car park, turn right down the hill and follow the lane round to the right. You'll immediately see a really attractive sheltered, grassy area with a cliff wall behind it. This is the most perfect place for a picnic at either end of the walk.

2 Keep following the lane to the right past a lovely house and then past the Goblin Combe Environment Centre. At this point in the walk, look across to the trees on your left, full of boughs of mistletoe. Keep going straight on, through the small metal gate beside the larger one with a sign saying Walnut Farm. Follow the path and soon enough you'll reach a wooden signpost which says: Welcome to Cleeve Wood.

3 Now you have a pleasant, slightly uphill walk through the woodland – an old-fashioned, dark green forest with fern, rocks and fallen trees combining to create a slightly mystical, damp, underwater feeling. You're walking between the high walls on either side of the gorge.

4 After half a mile (0.8km), you'll come through a gap in an ancient, dry stone wall. This marks the entrance to Goblin Combe Woodland.

5 Immediately to your left are some steps cut into the hillside and rising steeply into the gloom above you. It's these steps you need to climb. They rise quickly and the drop is sheer, so we don't recommend this to anybody who isn't reasonably fit, and the steps can be

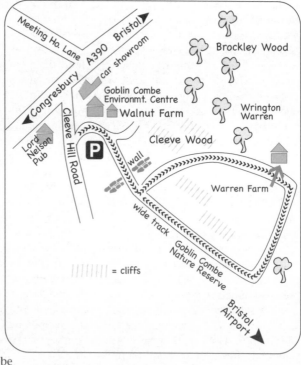

slippery so take care. The steps continue up the side of the gorge, sometimes followed by a few metres of flat walk where the path narrows away to little more than a rabbit run. Do not give up, you are going the right way!

6 Towards the top of the hill, you go through a gap in another tumbledown dry stone wall. (Why, one wonders did the landowners feel the need to go to the immense cost in manpower to build these walls right up here?) Keep the wall to your right as you follow the path which is, again, very narrow and not very clearly defined. When you cut through the wall again, you're nearly at the top.

7 Just a few more steps and suddenly you're out of the woods, hopefully in the sunshine, and standing on top of the world with the most breath-taking views in front of you. Up here you get a perfect view of aircraft passing almost within touching distance as they start their descent to the airport.

On a clear day you'll easily spot the Bristol Channel islands of Steep Holm and Flat Holm, and look way over the water to South Wales and the North Devon coastline. Turn slightly to your left, and Somerset stretches out in front of you, the Mendips in all their glory and the flatter land beyond. It is absolutely stunning and you'll understand why so many people think this is the most beautiful spot in England.

8 Turn left now and walk along the backbone of the ridge, a stony, rocky outcrop with, in summer, lovely wild flowers blooming in every crack and so many butterflies you'll lose count.

There's a pleasant grassy area beyond the rocky ridge which is a safe place to stop and rest and enjoy the views. The day we went, a buzzard was circling lazily overhead. In the olden days, the place was known as eagle gorge – slightly ironic given the aeroplanes which dominate the skies today.

9 It's hard to tear yourself away, but when you're ready to leave, take the top path to a wooden bar, and follow the yellow arrow to a grassy, tumpy track to the left (or you can walk through the overgrown meadow in front of you). Depending on the time of year you visit, you may smell wild honeysuckle, buddleia and lilac.

10 Soon the track meets another grassy track leading to the right downhill from Warren Farm. Follow the broad track, and it will lead you back down into the bottom of the gorge.

11 At the bottom, turn right, and, keeping right, follow the track which will eventually lead you back to the dry-stone wall where you started your ascent.

12 From here simply retrace your steps to the car park.

Wraxall

17

DISCOVERING A LONG-LOST BATHING POOL

Distance: About 4 miles (6.5 km).

Walking time: Allow 2–3 hours.

Suitability: Not suitable for buggies, push-chairs or wheelchairs.

Terrain: This walk is fine for children old enough to walk the whole way themselves. There's quite a lot to keep them interested along the way but it does get horrendously muddy after wet weather so wear your wellies.

GETTING THERE

Take the B3130 through Wraxall towards Nailsea. At the first mini roundabout go straight over, at the second turn left into Lodge Lane. This lane now winds its way past the Elms housing development on the left. Follow the lane straight across two roundabouts and then down into the countryside. (If you reach a third roundabout, you've gone too far.)

Keep going for about a mile as the lane winds down the hill until you're at the bottom of the valley surrounded by open fields.

Look for a gate just past a cottage on the left-hand side with a footpath marker pointing three different ways. There's room here to park several cars at the side of the road.

Dogs: With the usual provisos of keeping dogs on leads near sheep, this is a great walk for dogs.

Refreshments: Nothing anywhere on this walk and it's a long way to the nearest shop or pub so do take refreshments with you. If you want to make a day of it, there are some good family pubs within easy driving distance, including the famous Battle Axes at Wraxall, The Star at Tickenham and the excellent Farmhouse at Nailsea.

BACKGROUND

UNTIL THE TURN OF THE CENTURY, it's unlikely that many Bristol people had even heard of Wraxall, let alone known where it was. To most, it was little more than a string of cottages at the side of a busy commuter route set in spectacularly lovely countryside.

But in 2001 Lord Wraxall, who had lived alone in Tyntesfield, the huge Gothic mansion at the centre of the Estate which stretched from Portbury to Flax Bourton, died unmarried and the future of the estate was thrown into doubt.

There isn't space here to go into much detail about the background to the estate, and the Gibbs family who lived there, but they were a very interesting and rather unconventional crowd. Most of their money came from bird poo neatly proving the theory that where there's muck, there's brass. They took a huge gamble when they shipped their first cargo of guano, which is the droppings of sea birds, into Bristol from the rainless islets along the Pacific coast of South America but it was an instant hit with the gardeners of Britain. Within years it was Britain's most popular fertilizer and the Gibbs family fortune was guaranteed.

The first parts of Tyntesfield were built in 1863. In all, the house cost £70,000 which was less than one year's average profits from the guano-importing business.

Unusually, the magnificent Victorian country house survived the ensuing century and a half with its contents, gardens, park and estate buildings intact. When the full nature of what had been preserved was discovered after the reclusive Lord Wraxall's death, there was great excitement and a nationwide appeal to save the more historically important parts of the estate for posterity was launched. Eventually it passed into the care of the National Trust. Many of the estate cottages and parts of the land were, however, sold off.

You can look round much of the property and gardens courtesy of the National Trust. Most, but not all of it, is now accessible, and you can watch conservation work in progress. Visitors are welcome to turn up on open days and walk round themselves (there are, however, quite high admission charges for those who aren't members of the National Trust) but timed tickets are in operation – to check availability call: 0870 458 4500 or visit: www.nationaltrust.org.uk.

The rest of the estate is being put to good use, and large sections are now being used for public events. From 2006, new horse trials will take place on the estate and the North Somerset Agricultural Society bought a section of the land included in this walk for their annual agricultural show.

Most significantly, the estate is where the new Children's Hospice South West will be sited. The foundation stone was laid at Charlton Farm in September 2005, the ceremony marking the halfway point in the £15 million appeal. At the time of writing, it was planned that the hospice should open its doors officially early in 2007.

The new hospice is needed to complement facilities at the only existing children's hospice in the region, at Little Bridge House in Barnstaple. The management wanted to find a large site in a tranquil and beautiful environment that would offer a peaceful haven for children and their families. Charlton Farm is a Grade II listed building lying within the Tyntesfield parkland. It includes a farmhouse, which will be used as the main building, and several barns set in 150 acres of pastureland. Babe's Big Appeal to raise the necessary funding has been enthusiastically supported by the people of Bristol.

That's the background to the Tyntesfield estate, but early in 2005, an amazing new discovery was made. In a secluded corner of the area of land belonging to the North Somerset Agricultural Society, a Victorian open-air bathing pool was found.

It was a long way from the road, completely shielded by trees, and fed by a fresh-water spring. Very little information about the pool is available, but it is believed that it must have been used by the Gibbs family, and their friends, to relax and cool off on summer days. The late Lord Wraxall's great grand-parents, William and Matilda, had seven children and 18 grandchildren so the pool would certainly have been put to good use and was probably a favourite haunt of the little Gibbses.

Plans to restore and renovate the pool are being mooted, but for now, you can walk to it if you so wish. Hardly anybody knows its location and rediscovering it with your children is quite a magical experience. The pool is quite long and deep enough for swimming, and the spring ensures it is constantly topped up with water which even today looks crystal clear. An old pump still stands, presumably for the rinsing off of muddy feet, and it's easy to imagine the Victorian children swinging into the water from ropes tied to the branches of the surrounding trees.

There is a fence around the pool, and a life-ring, but it is very deep so don't let your children go anywhere near the edge.

1 Climb over the stile beside the gate and follow the edge of the field round to the left, keeping the hedge on your left. You'll go past some farm buildings and eventually come to a wooden footbridge over the stream to your left.

2 Cross the bridge and then turn right, walking beside the stream and keeping it to your right. There are very good views from here up to Tyntesfield and across the valley. This is one of those walks which changes dramatically with the seasons. The best views are to be had in winter, when the leaves have fallen and the estate buildings are visible on the hill to your left.

3 It's a relaxing, pleasant walk beside the stream, which bubbles obligingly. After a while, you'll see some derelict farm buildings up ahead of you and slightly to the left. Head for these. You'll need to climb over a gate to go into the old farm yard. It's a terrible shame that the farm is derelict as it's in the most perfect spot and must have been lovely when it was somebody's home. Don't go into any of the buildings, and don't be alarmed by some rather ghostly clanking and gurgling noises emerging from beneath the old pumphouse in the lower right-

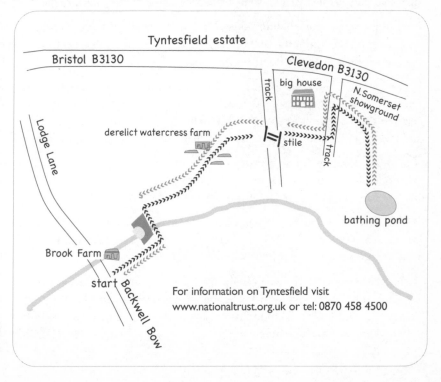

hand corner of the yard – these are particularly unnerving after heavy rain! You can also peep into a genuine well in the yard, which is only partially covered by a huge round slab. Needless to say, hold on tight to children and dogs.

4 This is one of those places where, having taken you to an obvious landmark, all footpath signs disappear completely. At this juncture, stop following the stream. There's a building at the far end of the yard directly opposite the gate where you came in.

5 Turn 90 degrees here and walk up the yard towards the track up to the road, with the building on your right and the old farmhouse on your left. At the top end of the yard, to the right of the track are two small stone buildings.

6 The footpath runs between these, and then follows the lower edge of the next field. Keep going around the field until you reach a gap in the hedge, more or less diagonally opposite the point where you came into the field.

7 If you go through the gap in the hedge, there is a track in front of you, and then, on the other side of the track directly opposite the gap in the hedge, is a stile. Take care because there is some barbed wire on either side of the stile.

8 Cross the stile and you'll find yourself in a small, rough field directly below a very grand house. Follow the edge of the field to your right and leave it through the gap between two large wooden gateposts.

9 Now turn left and walk up the gravelled track until you reach a gate on your right. At this point, you should pick up the yellow footpath marker arrows again. It's also an excellent spot for birdwatching, we saw two buzzards, a heron and a woodpecker while crossing the next field.

10 This is a big field, but cross it in a straight line heading for two wooden posts opposite. Go straight across the next field which takes you right up to the border of the land used for the agricultural shows.

11 Turn right here and walk down until you reach the bottom edge of the field you just crossed. Go a few steps to your right and then walk downhill with the trees to your left. The secret pool is in the middle of these trees.

12 It's back the same way you came once you've had enough of admiring the pool, but the views going in this direction are equally breath-taking. However, you might need some kind of incentive to keep the children motivated all the way back, so we would recommend the promise of a good meal at one of the local pubs.

Cadbury Camp

WONDERFUL VIEWS AND AN IRON AGE HILL FORT

Distance: About 1½ miles (3 km).
Walking time: 1–2 hours.
Suitability: Not suitable for buggies, pushchairs or wheelchairs.
Terrain: This isn't a walk for the faint-hearted – the hills are steep and much of the walk is on grass. If your children are too big to carry, they'll need to be willing to walk themselves and this really isn't one for elderly grandparents. It is, however, a good walk for dogs as long as they are kept under control around any livestock.
Parking: Tickenham village hall car park.
Refreshments and toilets: None. However there are some good, family-friendly pubs nearby. The Black Horse at Easton-in-Gordano and the Star at Tickenham are just a short distance away and there are cafés, shops and public toilets in nearby Nailsea.

GETTING THERE
Take the B3128 out of Bristol and turn right at the junction with the B3130, heading towards Clevedon. Slow down as you head into Tickenham Village, and turn right into the village hall car park.

THIS IS A LOVELY WALK AT ANY TIME OF YEAR, with panoramic views across Somerset and the Bristol Channel from the top of the hill. It's also a great place for bird and wildlife watching.

Although Cadbury Camp is an important historical site, and metaphorically just a stone's throw from the three north Somerset towns of Clevedon, Nailsea and Portishead, it's quite unusual to meet anybody on this walk.

Cadbury Camp is a huge, flat, hilltop circle with two steep mounds and ditches surrounding its perimeter. Cadbury means 'Cada's fort' and Cada was an early Anglo-Saxon name.

The camp was originally a late-iron age hill fort. The native Dobunni tribe dug out the ditches and threw back the soil to make the high banks which helped protect the fortress. The banks were then topped with a high timber fence, and a complicated entrance made it very difficult to attack. At that time, the surrounding flat lands would have been boggy marshes. The people lived in basic, wooden huts thatched with the reeds that still grow prolifically beside the Somerset rhines, and their animals would be kept in adjoining pens.

It's likely that people lived on Cadbury Camp for thousands of years. A bronze spearhead has been found up there, and the discovery of a small statuette indicates that it may have been the site of a Roman temple.

1 From the village hall car park, turn left and walk a short distance along the busy B3130. After a couple of minutes, you'll see a sign directing you towards a stile and a footpath between two houses. Follow the path to the top – it's narrow and gets quite steep. Climb over the stile and follow the yellow arrow up the steps and then up the very steep hill.

2 You rise so fast it's like being in an aeroplane. You'll probably find you need to keep stopping to catch your breath, so take the opportunity to turn round and soak up the views of the sky and the countryside. The church in the middle of the fields is the peculiarly named St Quiricus and St Julietta in Tickenham. As you continue to climb you can see beyond Nailsea and Clevedon as far as Crooks Peak and the Bristol Channel islands of Steep and Flat Holm. On really clear days, you can make out the coastline of north Devon in the distance.

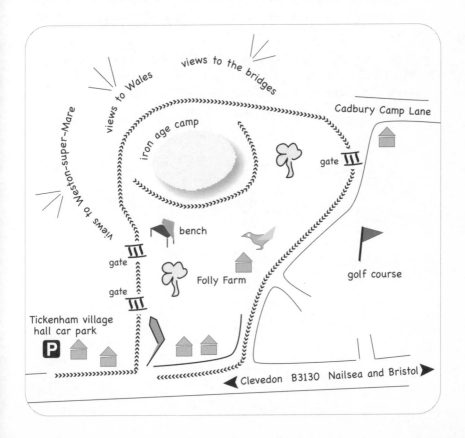

3 Eventually you'll reach a stile. Climb over and walk uphill along a path lined with gorse. At the top there's a strategically placed bench where you can rest your legs and enjoy the views.

4 With your back to the bench, follow the worn grass path over the two hilly mounds into the camp itself. It's a lovely, peaceful place and worth walking along the top of one of the perimeter mounds to make sure you don't miss any of the gorgeous views. This is a lovely picnic spot (providing the centre of the camp hasn't been commandeered by cattle!) and it's also an excellent place to pick blackberries in September.

5 Directly opposite the place where you first came into the camp, there's a break in the boundary mounds. You'll see a metal information board. With the board to your left, follow the path downhill, and climb over the stile at the bottom. Take the right-hand path and follow the stony lane downhill. When it becomes tarmac, turn right and go through the metal gate marked 'Public Bridleway'.

6 Now follow the pleasant path downhill, enjoying yet more lovely views across the woods, the valley and Tickenham Golf Club. When the path forks, follow the right-hand fork back down to the road. From here, simply follow the pavement back to the village hall car park.

Brean Down 19

WADING BIRDS AND WILD GOATS
AND A LOVELY BEACH

GETTING THERE

Brean Down, which is owned and managed by the National Trust, is about 8 miles (13km) from the M5, Junction 22. If you're coming from Weston-super-Mare, follow the signs to the hospital, then signs to Brean. It's a very winding and convoluted lane, but you will get there in the end.

Distance: About 3 miles (5km).

Walking time: Allow 2 hours.

Suitability: Not suitable for pushchairs or wheelchair users. Perfect for children old enough to walk the whole way themselves. The fort adds incentive and interest.

Facilities: There's a National Trust car park at the foot of the Down, together with a café, toilets and a free exhibition about the history and wildlife of the area. There are good, clean beaches at Brean and Berrow to the south of the Down within easy reach if you wanted to make the walk part of a family day out. There are also plenty of family-friendly pubs and restaurants in and around Brean.

Warning! The cliffs are dangerous – according to the signs at the bottom of the Down, around one dog a month is lost over the edge so it's safest to keep yours on a lead.

THIS IS A LOVELY WALK AROUND ONE OF THE MOST INTERESTING LANDMARKS of the Somerset coastline with plenty of features to explore and things to see.

Brean Down is the huge, limestone hill which juts out into the Bristol Channel just south of Weston-super-Mare. It is the last part of the chain of the Mendip Hills and was formed about 300 million years ago.

The Down reaches 100 metres above sea level at its highest point and has spectacular views over Weston, the Somerset levels and across the channel to the islands of Steep Holm, Flat Holm and over to South Wales.

Brean Down has been home to animals and people for around 10,000 years. Remains of mammoths and woolly rhinoceros have been found, as well as Stone Age burial mounds and a temple. It's easy to imagine what it must have been like living on the rock in the old days, because there are so few modern features up there.

Nowadays, the most impressive architectural feature is what's left of the fort, originally built to protect the Bristol Channel in 1865. The fort's history and some entertaining anecdotes can be found on the information boards and children and adults are welcome to explore the old buildings at the far tip of the Down. Volunteers open the officers' quarters and the gun magazines for visitors most Sunday afternoons between Easter and the end of September.

The wildlife is impressive. It is a great place to watch birds, especially when the tide goes out and oyster-catchers, redshanks, and others converge to feast on the mudflats. More entertaining for younger children are the wild and woolly goats which jump along the cliff edges.

1 From the car park, walk around the café and follow the path up to the steep steps which climb up the Down. This is a challenging climb! Once at the top, you'll need to stop to catch your breath and enjoy the views. Look out for a huge arrow painted onto the top of the hillside. During the Second World War, this arrow directed bomber planes to the practice range on the beach below.

2 Turn right at the top, and then left, taking the lower, better defined track along the northern side of the down. The views across the bay to Weston-super-Mare are breathtaking, no matter what the weather. The sea here has the second largest tidal movement in the world. The distance between high water and low water can be as much as three quarters of a mile (1.2km). The current at the tip of Brean Down is amazingly strong (about four knots).

3 The track leads past the site of what was to be a deep-water harbour at Brean Down. In the 1860s, foundation stones for a pier were laid, but the project was later abandoned after a fierce storm. These North Cliffs are a good spot for butterfly and bird watching.

4 Soon you reach Brean Fort, built in 1870 to protect the channel from French invaders (the French just having constructed a terrifying new kind of battleship). The Fort had seven big guns and was, incredibly, occupied by around 20 men and their families. It must have been very cosy! During the Second World War the fort was re-armed with bigger, better guns which had the capacity to sink ships even at the other side of the channel. It's well worth stopping to explore the fort, and to discover its connection with the bouncing bomb.

5 With your back to the fort, take the right-hand path across the grass back in the direction of the coast. Another good spot for soaking up the seascape, this is where Guglielmo Marconi set a new distance record for wireless transmissions to Lavernock Point in Wales in 1897. To your right are the remains of some ancient field systems.

6 It's a bit of a climb up to the highest point of the Down, more than 100 metres above sea level. To your right are the South Cliffs, covered with low-growing vegetation which has to cope with winds that can be quite strong even on a warm day. Look out for peregrine falcons and kestrels hunting on the Down.

As you head back along the southern side, enjoy the spectacular views of the coastline. This is where you'll see the wild goats hopping from outcrop to outcrop in a quite amazing manner. At the second highest point of the Down, you pass the spot where the Romans built a small temple in a site perfectly suited to enjoy sunset.

7 You can either go back down the steps or follow the path on down, past the brick gun emplacements used to provide training for soldiers in the Second World War (using targets in Weston bay), and the remains of the iron age hill fort built to defend the entrance to the River Axe. This leads you round to a gentle walk down to a gate at the bottom of the hill, and the path back to the café to enjoy a mug of tea or an ice-cream (or both). After this, we recommend a picnic on Brean's beautiful, sandy beach.

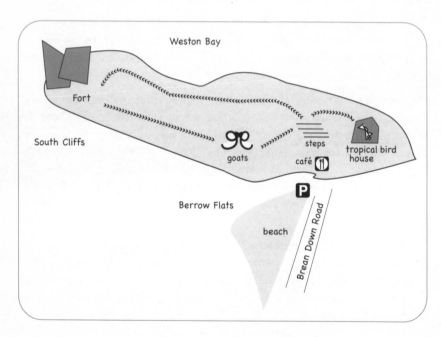

Poets' Walk

Poets' Walk

Poets' Walk

NOW DANCE THE LIGHTS ON LAWN AND LEA

GETTING THERE
From Bristol, go over the Cumberland Basin and leave the road by the David Lloyd sports centre. Follow the B3128 right to the end, turn right onto the B3130 and, when you reach Clevedon, follow the signs to the seafront. The Salthouse car park at the start of the walk is clearly marked.

Distance: About 1¹/₂ miles (2.5 km).
Walking time: 1 hour.
Suitability: Not suitable for wheelchair users. There are steps but they are shallow, so light pushchairs would be fine.
Terrain: This is an easy, gentle walk along metalled paths which makes it a good one for the winter months and quite suitable for elderly relatives too as there are plenty of benches en route. Any child aged three upwards should be able to manage this walk. Although it's along cliffs, there are fences all the way round. The views across the estuary are quite spectacular and change on a minute-to-minute basis depending on the light.
Dogs: No problem at all.
Parking: Pay-and-display car park.
Refreshments: The Salthouse playing fields to the right of the car park contain play equipment for different aged children and there's a miniature railway in the summer months. There's a kiosk at the top of the car park which sells drinks, ice creams and even hot food but it tends to be open only in the summer. On the other side of the playing fields are tennis courts, crazy golf, a small amusement arcade with toddler rides, and behind this are tea gardens with toilets. The Salthouse pub at the start of the walk has just been refurbished, welcomes families, has a large garden and terrace and serves food. We also thoroughly recommend the Little Harp pub behind the tennis courts which has a family area and which serves lovely, good value food all year round.
Toilets: Public toilets.

POETS' WALK IS A NATURE RESERVE and one of the best places to enjoy views across the Severn Estuary. On clear days, you're supposed to be able to make out the Millennium Stadium in Cardiff across the channel. The walk is named after the writers and poets who used to visit Clevedon. These included Coleridge and Tennyson, whose friend Arthur Hallam is buried in the twelfth-century churchyard of St Andrew's. John Betjeman was a friend of the Elton family and wrote an evocative piece about Clevedon in *First and Last Loves*.

The estuary is one of the largest in Europe and has the second highest tides in the world. It can be hard to imagine when you're staring out across the spectacular mudflats, but the waters of the estuary are home to 80 different kinds of fish and 10 billion shrimps (it must have been quite a job counting them!). There are also more than 50,000 migratory water birds and this walk is a very good way to spot some of them.

The cliff path was made by the unemployed in the 1930s. At the far end, past the church, is Wain's Hill, an iron-age hill fort. The remains of a defensive bank and ditch on the landward side of the promontory can still be made out. It is difficult to imagine what it must have been like living in the fort. The trees today are hunched over against the wind. Our iron-age ancestors must have been very tough. Another interesting feature is the 'pillow mound' which is where people used to farm rabbits in medieval times.

Clevedon itself is best known for its elegant Victorian pier which has been beautifully restored after it collapsed in 1970, ironically while it was undergoing safety tests. If you are feeling energetic, it's a pleasant walk from the Salthouse fields along to the pier, via the seafront which still boasts an old-fashioned Victorian bandstand.

1 Park in the pay-and-display car park, and you'll probably have to wait ten minutes while your children enjoy the play equipment beside it. Then follow the path past the toddlers' play area and veer left past the Salthouse pub. To your right is the marine lake. In Victorian times, seawater lakes were considered a cheap and effective way of providing visitors and residents with bathing facilities, particularly in areas where there were high, dangerous tides – like Clevedon. The lake enjoyed its heyday in the 1930s and many of Clevedon's older residents learned to swim there and have very fond memories. It has to be said, the lake does not look the least bit tempting nowadays.

2 Don't turn right, but follow the path up some shallow steps into the wood. Go up the first 19 steps, and then turn right. Soon you'll reach a circular seat and the first of a series of dramatic viewing points across the estuary and across the bay to Clevedon pier and the old, Victorian part of the town. A little further along is another dramatic lookout perched right on the edge of the cliff. The original viewpoint was built by a German called Conrad Finzel who made a fortune out of importing and processing sugar in Bristol and who lived in Clevedon. If you are very, very lucky you might spot a seal in the channel.

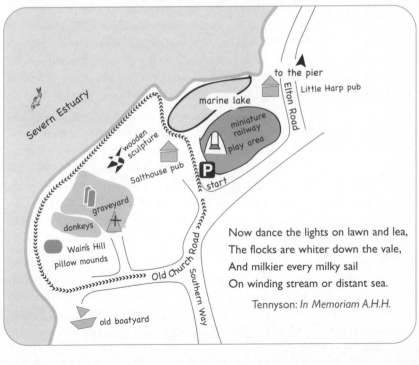

Now dance the lights on lawn and lea,
The flocks are whiter down the vale,
And milkier every milky sail
On winding stream or distant sea.

Tennyson: *In Memoriam A.H.H.*

3 At the next fork, you can either turn left and scramble up the grassy slope to the area above which has great views and is a good place for a picnic. Here, you'll find a wooden 'sculpture' – planks of wood sticking out of the ground rather like a shipwreck. Inscribed on them is a line from Tennyson's poem 'In Memoriam' dedicated to his friend Arthur Hallam, buried in the churchyard below.

4 Alternatively, go straight ahead keeping the church of St Andrew's and the graveyard to your left and the sea to your right. St Andrew was the patron saint of fishermen, and in olden times people used to light beacons along the ridge where the footpath now runs to warn ships away from the rocks below. This is the oldest church in Clevedon, and it is famous for its pagan connections. If you look closely you'll find images of the ancient Green Man, which implies that the existing 600-year-old church was built on the site of an even older sacred place. One of the graves in the churchyard is dedicated to Frederick Durbin, a Clevedon man so passionately opposed to slavery that he joined the American Federal army and was killed at the battle of Gettysburg in 1863. Even sadder is the tablet inside the church which reminds us of two young members of Clevedon's wealthy Elton family. Abraham, aged 14, and his 13-year-old brother Charles were swept away by the tide while playing off Birnbeck Island in Weston-super-Mare in 1819. Their bodies were discovered together, each brother had his arms wrapped around the other. This touching but tragic event is recalled in the inscription: 'The flood was stronger than their strength though not their love.' It is said that, since then, the spirits of the boys have warned other children away from Birnbeck Island, and anybody who has ever visited will know that there is always a strange chill in the air there.

5 Back to Poets' Walk... just past the graveyard is a well-worn field which is home to a group of very friendly donkeys. They are quite happy to be petted if they are close to the fence, but don't be startled by the noise if they start to bray! Further on, the land opens up into a second grassy area. This is Wain's Hill, the site of the old hill fort. It's a good place for a picnic, and the views from here are quite breathtaking. When the tide is out, the vast expanse of mud, rippling with patterns carved out by the sea, is beautiful and surreal. Little fishing boats lean stranded on the mud and hundreds of seabirds hunt by the shore.

6 The path curves down from here back down to sea level. At the bottom, you can turn right and follow the way past an old yard where several derelict boats stand sadly abandoned, or follow the path back through a wooden gate into Old Church Road, past the allotments and the entrance to the church, and back to the car park. It's a very quiet road and there's a good-sized pavement.

Berkeley

A BLOODY HISTORY, A CASTLE AND A BUTTERFLY HOUSE

Distance: About $1^1/_2$ miles (2.5 km).

Walking time: One hour or upwards, depending on how long you spend exploring the church and town.

Suitability: Because there are several stiles to be climbed, this walk is not suitable for buggies, pushchairs or wheelchairs. However, there are alternative, pavemented routes through the town which are accessible to all. This is a good walk for dogs, just look out for livestock.

Parking: There's a well signposted car park in the town and plenty of parking at the side of the main streets.

Refreshments: Lots of olde shoppes, cafés, restaurants and pubs.

Toilets: Public toilets in Berkeley.

There are plenty of things to do and see in the town itself. Most famous are, of course, Berkeley Castle www.berkeley-castle.com   tel: 01453 810332, the associated Butterfly House where you can see hundreds of beautiful, free-range butterflies and the Jenner Museum www.jennermuseum.com tel: 01453 810631, which is packed with displays and information about Edward Jenner, the man responsible for saving probably millions of lives by his research into smallpox and the invention of the preventative inoculation.

There really is enough to do and see to make Berkeley worth a whole day out in its own right, but there are lots of other attractions nearby including Slimbridge Wildfowl and Wetlands Centre, Cattle Country Adventure Park and Newark Park.

Berkeley Castle: www.berkeley-castle.com Tel: 01453 810332

Jenner Museum: www.jennermuseum.com Tel: 01453 810631

GETTING THERE
From the M5 head north on the A38 following signs to Berkeley and then brown signs to Berkeley Castle. It's about 20 minutes' drive from the M5.

THE HISTORIC MARKET TOWN OF BERKELEY AND THE VALE beyond which stretches picturesquely down to the River Severn (the view only spoiled by the ugly, concrete hulk that is Oldbury nuclear power station), are amongst the gems of south Gloucestershire. The castle is just like a castle should be, a great, ancient rambling structure with lots of turrets and chimneys and leaded windows, looking out over Elizabethan gardens, an historic churchyard and some lovely countryside. The castle dates back to 1117 and is still home to the Berkeley family who gave their name to numerous high profile places including Berkeley Square in London and Berkeley University in California.

The castle is most famous for being the scene of the brutal murder of Edward II in 1327. The king, son of Edward I, did nothing particularly heroic and was not a popular man. After being held prisoner in Berkeley Castle for 18 months, he was eventually killed in an extremely unpleasant manner with a red hot poker. The poor man's screams were heard in the village of Berkeley and are, apparently, still heard there today.

The castle is well worth a visit. Part of the interior still looks as it did when Edward II was prisoner there, and children will enjoy the excitement and intrigue of exploring such a huge, historic place. From an adult perspective, there are collections of tapestries, furniture and rare paintings by, primarily, English and Dutch masters in the state apartments. You can also go into the Great Hall where the barons of the west country met in 1215 before going to Runnymede to force King John to put his seal to Magna Carta. Outside, you can still see Queen Elizabeth I's bowling green. The outer bailey overlooks the New Kennels, home to the Berkeley Hunt since 1730. The Butterfly House is set in the walled garden next to the car park.

The castle and Butterfly House are only open at certain times during the winter months, and it's best to check on the telephone number given earlier, or via the website, at any time of year before setting out.

1 If you're starting from somewhere in the town, find the High Street and walk along it until you see the sign to the Jenner Museum. Edward Jenner was the vicar's son. In 1823 he discovered the power of vaccination and treated his patients here.

2 Take the path on the left and you can either stop off to explore the museum, or carry on to the Church of St Mary the Virgin. You need to take the path directly across the church yard, but if you have time, stop for a look inside the church which is so steeped in history you can almost taste it.

One unusual aspect of the church is that its tower stands totally separate to the main building which dates back to 1100. John Trevisa, a translator of the first Bible into English was vicar here in 1385 and in 1399 the coalition between Henry of Lancaster and Edmund, Duke of York against Richard II was ratified on the site. Amongst scores of interesting features inside the church is the alabaster tomb of Lord Thomas of Berkeley, who died in 1361 and his second wife Lady Katharine, who died in 1385.

Thomas was Lord of Berkeley at the time of Edward II's murder, and it's quite strange to look into the faces of two people who must have known the unlucky king. There's a notice beside the tomb which tells of Thomas's heroic military exploits. Katharine was the founder of the nearby Katharine Lady Berkeley School at Wotton-under-Edge. On the window ledges nearby are three small stone statues. These are three of the couple's sons who died as babies, Maurice, Edmund and Thomas.

Lots of interesting people are buried outside the church too, and the graveyard has some incredibly ornate headstones. Edward Jenner is buried here, along with Dicky Pearce, England's last court jester who died in 1728, and George and Mary Thorpe, grandchildren of the founders of Berkeley in Virginia, America.

3 By now, your children will be going into historical overload, so go through the gate at the opposite side of the churchyard, turn immediately right and then left and follow the road. There's a good pavement and you'll cross several streams and a river.

4 You pass stables on the left, and might see the horses exercising. A little further on is an interesting crenellated gothic house, and you then go past the Berkeley Estate Office and the Salutation pub. You might like to stop at the Salutation for refreshment. There's a nice garden outside. After this, you soon reach a lovely, old-fashioned village green. Follow the track to the left and you

Edward Jenner

Edward Jenner trained in medicine and was always intrigued by folklore which said that milkmaids who'd had cowpox, a mild disease, could not catch smallpox which, at the time, killed one in five of the population. In May 1796, Jenner scratched material infected with cowpox into the skin of James Phipps, his gardener's son. When he had recovered, Jenner tried to give him smallpox, but Phipps was immune. It was very brave of James Phipps to allow Jenner

to do this — if the experiment had gone wrong, he would almost certainly have died so you can appreciate why Jenner would have rewarded his servant's trust and faith with a cottage.

As a direct result of this original experiment, the World Health Organisation finally eradicated smallpox after a massive immunology programme in 1980.

Jenner made other important medical discoveries and was probably the first person to fly a hot air balloon in Britain, from Berkeley Castle. He also discovered the first Plesiosaurus fossil on nearby Stinchcombe Hill. If you visit the Jenner Museum, you can still see his study and the thatched hut in the garden where he vaccinated the poor, free of charge.

walk past the old village pump and some pretty cottages. There are horses everywhere, in fields and stables.

5 With Little Green Cottage on your right, follow the path forwards, enjoying the lovely views. All the footpath signs disappear at this point, but don't panic. Don't turn into the farmyard but keep following the track. It can get very muddy after rain. You'll cross the river again and then climb over the wooden stile beside a metal gate. Keep the river to your left, and follow it into the next field. This is a fantastic way to see the Castle, which will now come into view. You simply can't enjoy this view in any other way.

6 Walk across this second field keeping the river to your left and cross into the next field. The castle is now right in front of you and you can see the terraced gardens, ornamental trees, and lovely, higgledy piggledy mass of windows and chimneys.

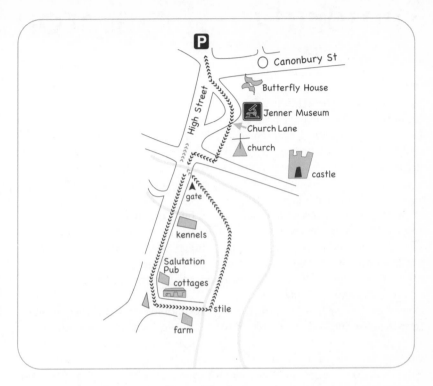

7 You are now in a very large, grassed field. Head across the field towards the white gate diagonally to your right. Close by, to the left, you'll see the stile set in the metal gate which takes you back out onto the road you walked down some time ago.

8 If you turn right and walk straight along the road, you'll find yourself back in the centre of the town. There are interesting houses and cottages to left and right. It's worth taking a quick diversion up Church Lane on the right. Here you'll see the cottage which Edward Jenner gave to James Phipps, the first person ever to be vaccinated against smallpox.

Slimbridge to Frampton

A PRETTY VILLAGE AND A ONCE MIGHTY CANAL

22

Distance: 8 miles (13km).

Walking time: At least 4 hours.

Suitability: Not suitable for buggies, pushchairs or wheelchairs.

Terrain: This is a long walk and suitable only for older children who enjoy a good ramble. Despite its length, it is almost completely flat, which means it's not strenuous, and as more than half the walk is either on tarmac roads, pavements, or a very well kept canal path, it's an easy walk at any time of year (although it may be muddy in parts in winter).

The first section is through farmland where the paths are not very well marked and this is not as picturesque or as interesting as the second section. If you wanted, you could just do the Frampton/Church End loop which is only about a mile and a half and takes in a section of the canal (see page 104).

Alternatively, you could omit this loop from the longer walk, but it would be a shame not to explore Frampton.

Dogs: Dogs will be fine. Some fields might contain livestock and you'll need to keep them on the lead at the side of the canal, but there's nowhere they can't go.

Parking: Free on-street parking.

Refreshments: There are pubs at Frampton, and a good tea shop which is open all week, but otherwise you'll be hard pressed to find refreshments. You may decide to take something to drink with you.

Toilets: No public toilets. Facilities available for clients of the pubs or tea shop.

GETTING THERE

From Bristol, either follow the A38 up past Thornbury and Berkeley until you reach the turn-off for Slimbridge or take the M5 North, leaving at Junction 14. Turn right onto the A38 and follow the signs for the Slimbridge Wildfowl and Wetlands Trust. There is plenty of on-street parking in Slimbridge, or there is a small, unmarked car park opposite the church.

BACKGROUND

THIS IS A WALK THROUGH A DIFFERENT KIND OF COUNTRYSIDE, the flat expanses that flank the Severn Estuary and link the two exquisite villages of Slimbridge and Frampton.

After looping round Frampton, the walk then takes you back to your starting point along the side of the Gloucester and Sharpness Canal. This is absolutely nothing like the Kennet and Avon Canal featured in the Dundas Aqueduct walk. This canal is the daddy of canals and was once the broadest, deepest canal in the world! It's probably at least four times as wide as the Kennet and Avon, and the experience of walking beside it is completely different.

The canal links the docks at Gloucester with those at Sharpness on the Severn. It's 16 miles (26km) long, originally had 16 bridges (it currently has 17) and is 5m deep. When it was built it was 6m feet deep, because it needed to accommodate the keels of big sailing ships, but as they gradually stopped using the canal, ˙nobody bothered to dredge the bottom. Although it is 16 miles (26km) long, it only has one lock which is testament to the flatness of the land through which it passes.

It must have taken an awful lot of men many months to dig out the huge canal, and work was eventually completed in 1827. For decades, the canal was extremely busy and of huge industrial importance. Before the warehouses and docks were built at Sharpness, boats would use the canal to reach Gloucester, either unloading there or continuing along the canal network into the Midlands.

Right up until the 1960s, the canal was used by tanker barges carrying oil and petroleum products. The docks at Sharpness are still thriving, but these days the canal is mainly used by pleasure craft, including narrowboats and two craft which belong to the National Waterways Museum in Gloucester Docks. These are the *Queen Boadicea II* which runs 45-minute trips up and down the Canal (you may well see her rippling up the water during your walk) and the *King Arthur* which runs all-day trips up the River Severn to Tewkesbury, and between Gloucester and Sharpness.

The canal is very important for another reason. It supplies the city of Bristol with half its drinking water. The water is taken into the canal at Gloucester docks, and flows along it, feeding the docks at Sharpness before being collected and channelled into Bristol Water's intake at Purton.

This walk starts at the village of Slimbridge, which lies close to the world famous Wildfowl and Wetlands Trust. There are plenty of walks to do at the WWT and it merits a whole day out in its own right, so we wouldn't recommend combining a visit with a walk. However, the village of Slimbridge is exceptionally pretty. The church, with its tall, graceful spire, is particularly beautiful, and is probably the best example in the county of the Early Gothic style of the thirteenth century. Although there isn't an awful lot else in the village, the houses and cottages are all very pretty.

Frampton, at the other end of the

walk, is a gorgeous, rambling old Cotswold town with what is said to be the longest village green in England, two duck ponds, and the spectacular Frampton Court, built in 1731 for Richard Clutterbuck, an official of the Bristol Customs House. There are some lovely houses on the green, and at the side of the road are cottages some of which, unlike those at Castle Combe, are slightly ramshackle and all the more charming for it! As you walk along you can see hens and cockerels

pecking around the washing lines and runner-bean pyramids in the gardens, snoozing cats on shed roofs, some gorgeous displays of English cottage gardenry, and we even met a very sociable rare breed pig. It reminded us of the landscapes in *The Darling Buds of May* (even though that was set in Essex!).

In between Frampton and Slimbridge is the attractive, secluded, and very prosperous hamlet of Church End. The houses are the sort which make you wish you'd won the lottery. The fourteenth-century parish church of St Mary the Virgin is huge and graceful, sitting in a large yard just a stone's throw from the Sharpness Canal.

It's hard to imagine now, but 200 years ago, this sleepy hamlet would have been very close to a huge industrial centre. Before the canal was built, there was a busy wharf on the tidal creek of the Severn Estuary with a tannery and brickworks. Scores of people were employed there, and every day vessels would load and unload their cargoes at the creek, before continuing on their journeys. Now, of course, it's difficult to imagine anywhere more rural or peaceful.

1 Starting from the main road through the village, opposite the church, turn left and you'll soon come to the post office. Turn right onto the marked path at the side of the building, go over a gate and follow the arrows through the field with the fence on your right.

2 Go over a stile and bear left across the next field, where you can still see the undulations of the old, medieval strip-farming. To your left you can see across the estuary to the hills of Wales and to your right are the Cotswolds.

3 Go over another stile and carry on ahead, between two fences. At the end of the field, bend right and go over a stile on the left. Keep the ditch and fence to your right and carry on until you reach a lane.

4 Here, go right and immediately left through a kissing gate and follow the wide track over a bridge across the river. Keep on the track and take the stile behind the pumping station. (nb: as we passed behind the pumping station, it suddenly growled into action, which was quite noisy and quite scary but apparently quite normal, so don't be alarmed if this happens to you.)

5 Keep following the river, until you cross a little stream via a concrete bridge. (Annoyingly, at this point all pointers and arrows disappear. If you are in doubt about which path you should be taking, just aim to keep going straight ahead and don't be tempted to divert along what look like better-used paths to the left.) Follow the path immediately ahead. There are some young trees to your left.

6 Keep going through the fields, when you see some pylons on your left, carry on ahead, up the hill following the grassy track. Carry on in a straight line until you reach a wooded area enclosed for breeding pheasants. With the hedge on your left, follow the track forward until you reach the next field. Now you should see some farm buildings in front of you, and a church to your far left.

7 Go over the gate and follow the path to your left around the edge of the field until you reach a big green metal barn. Go over the stile here, and walk forwards between the buildings to the lane. Turn right and follow the road into Church End.

8 Turn left and you'll pass the war memorial and the church. There's a narrow stile at the end of the church wall, turn right and now you can walk towards Frampton between an avenue of huge horse-chestnut trees. This is excellent conker-hunting territory in mid-September. At the end of the field is a lych-gate – this must have been the route to the church from Frampton.

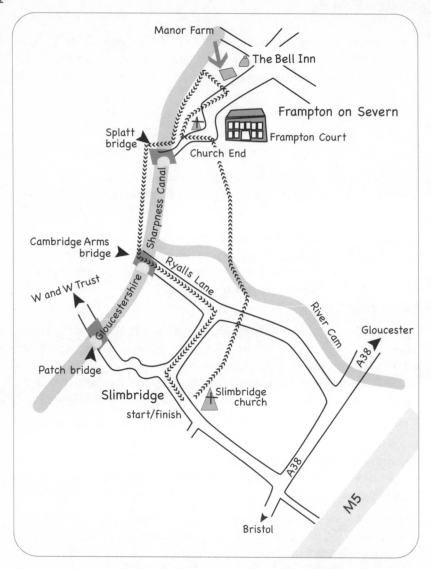

9 Go through the lych-gate and follow the road straight ahead into the town. There's a little café on the left-hand side and a little further up is the Three Horseshoes pub which also serves food.

10 Keep going up the main street. After the pub, the town peters out, and you're walking beside the long village green. You'll pass two ponds (fishing allowed by local residents only) on your right, and see the entrance to Frampton Court on the other side of the road. Soon after this, you'll reach Manor Farm on your left. Immediately beyond the stable buildings is a signed footpath.

11 Follow the path through the paddocks behind the stables, and then keep the fence on your left and follow the path over a plank bridge. Keep to the left side of the next field, and follow the path to the far left-hand side corner, where it goes into some trees, and then banks uphill. Here you'll need to stop and enjoy the breath-taking view of the Sharpness Canal in front of you, and beyond that the Severn Estuary.

12 Turn left and follow the footpath alongside the canal until you reach Splatt swing bridge, which isn't far away. Beside the bridge is a very elegant bridgeman's house. Eight of the canal's bridges have such houses beside them, the front door flanked by Doric columns. Each is built to the same specification with a living room, a bedroom and a scullery at the back. Now the bridges which cross the canal are made of steel, but originally they were wooden. It was important to have a bridgeman on duty at all hours of the day and night to swing the bridges so that vessels could carry on down the canal.

13 Cross the bridge, turn left, and carry on down this side of the canal. There's plenty to see – canal boats, pleasure craft, swans, ducks and, over to your right, the Severn Estuary. Keep walking until you reach the next bridge, called the Cambridge Arms bridge and cross the canal again.

14 You come out into a very quiet lane flanked by more big houses. Follow the lane, and take the first turning right. You'll see Slimbridge church spire over to your left. Follow the lane right to the end, turn left at the T-junction and you'll find yourselves back where you started.

Frampton on Severn

A SHORT WALK BY THE SHARPNESS CANAL

23

Distance: $1^{1}/_{2}$ miles (2.5 km).

Walking time: 1 hour.

Suitability: Not suitable for buggies, pushchairs or wheelchairs.

A shorter version of the Slimbridge/Sharpness walk which includes the picturesque town of Frampton on Severn, the church at Church End and the Sharpness Canal.

Dogs: Dogs will be fine. Some fields may contain livestock and you'll need to keep them on the lead at the side of the canal, but there's nowhere they can't go.

Parking: On-street parking.

Refreshments: There are two pubs at Frampton, the Bell and the Three Horseshoes, and a good tea shop which is open all week.

Toilets: For customers of the pubs and the tea shop.

GETTING THERE

From Bristol, either follow the A38 up past Thornbury and Berkeley until you reach the B4071 turn, or take the M5 North leaving at Junction 13. Turn left onto the A38 and then right following the signposts to Frampton.

BACKGROUND

THIS WALK STARTS AT THE TOWN OF FRAMPTON ON SEVERN which is one of the most picturesque towns in this part of the world. It is full of lovely houses of all types, periods and sizes. There are plenty of parking spaces.

The Sharpness Canal is a much shorter walk than the one listed previously by simply walking the top loop. We've reversed the directions just to ring the changes a bit! You will have plenty of time to explore the town.

THE WALK FRAMPTON ON SEVERN

1 At the very end of the long, straight street that runs through the village green, you'll find a church lych gate. Go through this and walk between the chestnut trees down towards the church ahead of you and slightly to your left. This is the church of St Mary the Virgin at Church End.

2 When you reach the church, turn right and head for the gate which takes you to Splatt swing bridge. Here you'll have good views of the spectacular Gloucestershire and Sharpness canal in both directions, and unless you're very unlucky, there'll be an interesting selection of longboats and pleasure craft moored up beside the bridge. Don't cross the bridge, instead turn right and walk alongside the canal, keeping the water to your left.

3 After a pleasant stroll, you'll pick up a footpath marker directing you to the right. There are sporadic markers from this point taking you to Manor Farm. If in doubt, just keep the hedge to your right. Soon you'll reach some paddocks and you'll see the farm buildings in front of you. The footpath runs to the right of the stable-block and brings you back out on to the road.

4 Now turn right and enjoy the picturesque street through this delightful Cotswold town. There are lots of things for children to enjoy, including some large duck ponds. If before you head back, you turn to your left, at the far end is the Bell Inn, good for a drink or a meal. Alongside is Bell Farm, where you can see pygmy goats, Jacob's sheep, Gloucester Old Spot pigs and Shetland ponies.

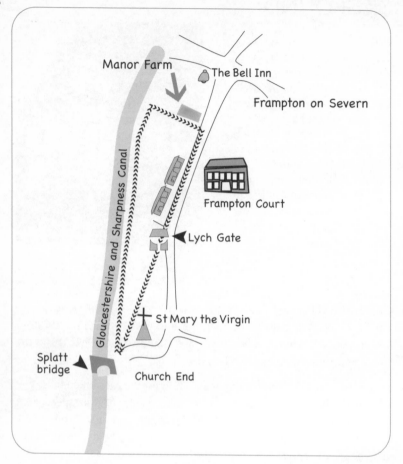

Manor Farm
The Bell Inn
Frampton on Severn
Gloucestershire and Sharpness Canal
Frampton Court
Lych Gate
St Mary the Virgin
Splatt bridge
Church End

5 As you walk back to your starting point you will pass the Frampton Cricket Club pavilion with, in front of it, probably the smallest cricket ground you will ever see. The road passes just a few yards from the wicket area in the middle. The boundaries on either side are so short that what would normally be four runs counts as just two, and a hit for six counts for just four. Across on the left, you can't miss the lovely Frampton Court and, in the gardens behind the high wall, its lovely Gothick Orangery.

6 Just keep going in a straight line and eventually you'll find yourself back where you started.

Castle Combe

DR DOLITTLE'S VILLAGE

GETTING THERE
Castle Combe is a way out of Bristol but it's worth the journey. Take the M4 East and get off at Junction 18 (Bath turn off). Take the A46 North (towards Stroud) and after about 2 miles (3km) turn right onto the B4040 towards Acton Turville. From here you should pick up the signs for Castle Combe, just make sure you get on to the B4039 which will take you into the village. There's a well-signposted car park above the village. Lots of people do drive into Castle Combe and park at the side of the road but it really does spoil the look of the place!

Distance: Shorter route 2 miles (3.2km).
Longer route 6 miles (9.5km).
Walking time: Shorter route $1\frac{1}{2}$ - 2 hours.
Longer route allow 4 hours.
Suitability: Not suitable for buggies, pushchairs or wheelchairs.
Terrain: We have given you two options for this walk and although the second option is quite long, it is an easy walk, with no really big hills, and relatively good paths all the way. There are some small stretches of road; most are fairly quiet but there is a small stretch walking along the A420 which is a fast road. Children who like walking shouldn't find this too arduous although it's probably best to be well stocked with drinks and snacks. If you have relatives or friends visiting from other parts of the country, Castle Combe is a good place to show off and you can always just potter around the village if you don't feel like walking far.
Dogs: Not the best walk for dogs, but so long as they don't mind being on the lead through the village, the golf course and the roads, they'll be happy.
Parking: Pay-and-display car park at the start of the walk or very limited parking on the road leading into the village.
Refreshments: There are a couple of really nice pubs in the village and a smattering of tea shops, but no 'takeaway' shops selling drinks, sweets or food.
Toilets: There are public toilets in the village.

CASTLE COMBE IS SAID TO BE THE PRETTIEST VILLAGE IN ENGLAND, and it probably deserves the title. It is exactly the sort of village that sums up all that's sweetest about rural England – a friendly, olde worlde pub with sloping floors and good beer, flowers tumbling out of windowboxes, an ancient market cross, birdsong, a picturesque stream with bossy parent ducks marshalling fluffy brown ducklings, and, one imagines, lacy doilies on the well-polished tables behind the mullioned cottage windows, tea brewed in silver pots and honey served on crumpets.

Like its sister village of Lacock, there is something ever so slightly artificial about Castle Combe. It is undeniably something of a museum piece, but there's nothing wrong with preserving a piece of living history in its entirety. In the summer, the narrow streets are full of tourists with cameras. There are plenty of little arty shops, and people take their drinks and ice creams over to the thirteenth-century, canopied market cross where they relax and socialise. The buildings are made of Cotswold stone and the village was the setting for the original *Doctor Dolittle* film. Since then it's been used as the backdrop for numerous films and TV programmes.

The village got its name from a castle that used to stand on the high ground above the golf course. After many years, the castle was demolished and the stone was used to build the houses in the village.

You can tell that this used to be a prosperous village by the high-quality workmanship on the buildings. Castle Combe grew rich thanks to the skill of the many professional weavers who used to live in the cottages. They perfected a thick, red cloth which was regarded as one of the best and most desirable in Europe and which is still used on the tunics of the guards outside Buckingham Palace.

The market cross was originally where the merchants and weavers would meet to trade wool.

Castle Combe prospered until the industrial revolution when its own weaving industry closed down almost overnight. Massive factories with large weaving machines could produce much more cloth much more quickly and much more cheaply. Yet although the industrial revolution killed off Castle Combe, it also helped preserve it. The village stayed in a timewarp, unchanged, until it was re-discovered in the 1950s and reinvented itself as a tourist attraction.

There's plenty to see in the village. Look out for the Pound, a walled enclosure on the right-hand side of the road as you head towards the old village. Animals which wandered off were kept here until their owners paid a fine to take them home.

The village museum is on the same side of the road and contains a history of the village and some interesting artefacts. It's a small museum, and used to be a chapel school room.

The Dower House was Dr Dolittle's house in the 1966 film, and of course there's the market cross.

I should also mention Castle Combe racetrack which is a must-see for racing enthusiasts. Most weekends there are vehicles with either two or four wheels making lots of noise on the track. You can also go motor-karting at Castle Combe should you feel so inclined and there's a skidpan.

The exquisite, upmarket town of Tetbury (much favoured by the Royals) and Westonbirt Arboreteum, home of the national tree collection, beautiful at any time of year but breathtaking in autumn, are also nearby.

THE WALK CASTLE COMBE

1 From the car park, turn right down the hill towards Castle Combe Village. At the junction, ignore the road on the left which goes down into the village, and take the right fork. Walk a short distance down the road until you see a small road on the right, and a row of cottages, signposted Nettleton Shrub.

2 Walk up this road to the top and then go over the stile. The golf course will lie to your right. Walk down hill to the wall and then bear right, keeping the wall to your left. You will come to a stile on your left, marked with a yellow arrow, but don't take this path (this leads you into the village). Instead bear right, with the wall on your left and follow the wall to a bridge, which you may recognise from *Doctor Dolittle*. Go over the bridge and fork left at the fourth tee, as indicated by a public footpath sign. Keep the stream on your right and go through the kissing gate in the wall.

3 Go a few metres up the track and then turn left between two mill buildings (this is Nettleton Mill). Now the stream is on your left. Follow it until you reach a stone bridge, where you cross back over to the other side.

4 Now you need to walk up a fairly steep hill, through several fields keeping in an almost straight line until you reach a road. Turn left and walk along the road past Shrub Farm. After a while, another road meets the one you're walking along on your left-hand side.

5 If you want to take the shorter walk, turn left at this junction, signposted Castle Combe, and follow the road down the hill to the village. You will find yourself at the bottom end of Castle Combe. Continue on this road past the market cross on your left, back to the car park.

6 Alternatively, for the longer walk, as soon as you meet the road leading into Castle Combe, start looking out for a marked path on your right. You will see a public footpath sign to Ford. Follow this path through some woodland, cross a stile and go straight on to the post in the middle of the field. Fork right downhill until you reach the fence, and follow it downhill to the stream. Cross the stream and keep going in the same direction as before, following the line of the valley until you reach a stile beside a house. Go over the stile and turn right down the track to the road.

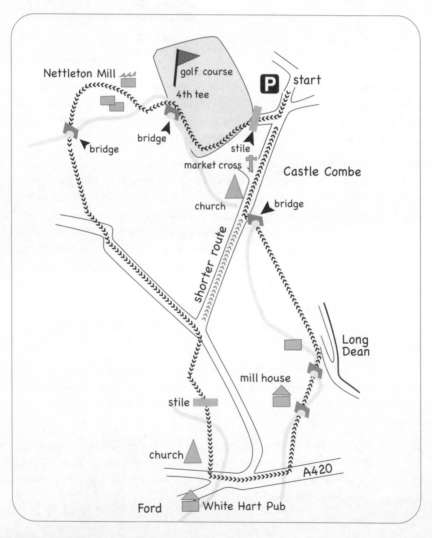

(If, by now, you are feeling in need of refreshment, you are a stone's throw from a very nice pub called the White Hart – it's only a few yards out of your way, just turn right and cross over the road.)

7 Turn left along the road and keep going, past the road to Castle Combe on your left-hand side, over the bridge and soon you'll see a path on the left.

Warning! This is a fast and busy road. The grass verge is fairly wide but at the bridge it becomes very narrow and children should be carefully supervised at all times.

8 Cross the stile and walk across the field to the woodland and the stream. Keep the stream on your left until you reach the bridge. Cross the stream and then cross back again after the mill. Keep the stream on your left until you come to a stile. Cross over the stile onto the track and turn right to Long Dean.

9 Take the public footpath signposted left. Follow the track uphill, past the mill on your left-hand side, and uphill to a couple of stiles. Now you have a lovely walk through patchy woodland, with gorgeous views down to the stream/river on your left. This is a very quiet, secluded path, and no matter how many tourists are in Castle Combe, none of them ever seem to come out here!

10 Just keep going in a straightish line until eventually you walk downhill and finally come out at a stone bridge. Now you're back at the bottom end of Castle Combe. Cross the bridge, and turn right up through the village to the market cross. Here, fork right and you'll find yourself back at the car park.

The Children's Bristol Series

www.childrensbristol.co.uk

Children's Bristol
Edited by John Sansom

This new, expanded edition of Bristol's best loved family guide is essential reading for anyone with children to bring up or entertain. Its opening chapters outline Bristol's fascinating history and its great maritime heritage. There are chapters on things to do, bright ideas for children's parties, family outings, places to visit in and around the city, to a radius of about 40 miles.

There are special chapters on animals and birds, historic places, museums, Roman remains, caves and even where to look for ghosts.

288 pages and fantastic value at £8.50.

Beastly Bristol

The streets of Bristol are full of animals, birds, insects and fish. All you have to do is look around, as Julian Lea-Jones shows in his fabulous new book Beastly Bristol. This fun book contains an A-Z of Bristol beasts, two location maps, a quiz and a gazetteer of places where you can see an astonishing 248 creatures.

From aardvarks to zebras, this wonderful gallery of animal forms is there to be enjoyed by children of all ages.

80 pages packed with fabulous colour and black and white illustrations. Just £6.95.

Children's Hospice South West

All our guides support this great charity. For every copy of *Children's Bristol* sold, we are donating 75p to the hospice; and 25p for every copy sold of *Beastly Bristol* and *24 Family Walks in and around Bristol*.